CW00669970

DEATH
— FOR —
DINNER
COOKBOOK

DEATH
— FOR —
DINNER
COOKBOOK

60 Gorey-Good, Plant-Based
Drinks, Meals & Munchies Inspired
by Your Favorite Horror Films

ZACH NEIL

ROCK
POINT

Inspiring | Educating | Creating | Entertaining

Brimming with creative inspiration, how-to projects, and useful information to enrich your everyday life, quarto.com is a favorite destination for those pursuing their interests and passions.

© 2022 by Quarto Publishing Group USA Inc.
Text © 2022 Zach Neil
Photography © 2022 Quarto Publishing Group USA Inc.

First published in 2022 by Rock Point, an imprint of The Quarto Group,
42 West 36th Street, 4th Floor, New York, NY 10018, USA
T (212) 779-4972 F (212) 779-6058 www.Quarto.com

All rights reserved. No part of this book may be reproduced in any form without written permission of the copyright owners. All images in this book have been reproduced with the knowledge and prior consent of the artists concerned, and no responsibility is accepted by producer, publisher, or printer for any infringement of copyright or otherwise, arising from the contents of this publication. Every effort has been made to ensure the credits accurately comply with information supplied. We apologize for any inaccuracies that may have occurred and will resolve inaccurate or missing information in a subsequent reprinting of the book.

Rock Point titles are also available at discount for retail, wholesale, promotional and bulk purchase. For details, contact the Special Sales Manager by email at specialsales@quarto.com or by mail at The Quarto Group, Attn: Special Sales Manager, 100 Cummings Center Suite, 265D, Beverly, MA 01915, USA.

10 9 8 7 6 5 4 3 2 1

ISBN: 978-1-63106-785-3

Library of Congress Control Number: 2022931113

Group Publisher: Rage Kindelsperger
Creative Director: Laura Drew
Managing Editor: Cara Donaldson
Senior Editor: Erin Canning
Cover Design and Illusration: Marisa Kwek
Interior Design and Layout: Silverglass
Photography: Charlie Chalkin and Tim O'Grady
pp. 14–15, George Rinhart/Corbis via Getty Images; p. 21, AF archive/Alamy Stock Photo; p. 25, Movie Poster Image Art/Getty Images; p. 27, Michael Ochs Archive/Getty Images; p. 32, Universal History Archive/UIG via Getty Images; pp. 34–35, Warner Brothers/Getty Images; p. 45: Movie Poster Image Art/Getty Images; p. 49: Michael Ochs Archive/Getty Images; p. 56, United Artists/Getty Images; p. 64, Universal History Archive/UIG via Getty Images; p. 67, Compass International Pictures/Getty Images; p. 73, Alba Photo/Shutterstock; p. 74, LMPC via Getty Images; p. 77, Everett Collection, Inc./Alamy Stock Photo; pp. 78–79, Warner Brothers/Getty Images; p. 87, LMPC via Getty Images; p. 90, AF archive/Alamy Stock Photo; pp. 96–97, Pictorial Parade/Getty Images; p. 98, LMPC via Getty Images; p. 101, Warner Brothers/Getty Images; p. 107, Universal History Archive/UIG via Getty Images; p. 111, Universal History Archive/UIG via Getty Images; p. 112, Bettman via Getty Images; p. 114, Universal History Archive/UIG via Getty Images; pp. 120–121, Movie Poster Image Art/Getty Images; p. 125, LMPC via Getty Images; p. 133, AF archive/Alamy Stock Photo; p. 134, LMPC via Getty Images; p. 136, LMPC via Getty Images; p. 138, Movie Poster Image Art/Getty Images

Food Styling: Nicole Pensabene

Printed in China

This publication has not been prepared, approved, or licensed by the author, producer, or owner of any motion picture, television program, book, game, blog, or other work referred to herein. This is not an official or licensed publication. We recognize further that some words, models names, and designations mentioned herein are the property of the trademark holder. We use them for identification purposes only.

This book provides general information. It should not be relied upon as recommending or promoting any specific diagnosis or method of treatment for a particular condition, and it is not intended as a substitute for medical advice or for direct diagnosis and treatment of a medical condition by a qualified physician. Readers who have questions about a particular condition, possible treatments for that condition, or possible reactions from the condition or its treatment should consult a physician or other qualified healthcare professional.

The Quarto Group denounces any and all forms of hate, discrimination, and oppression and does notcondone the use of its products in any practices aimed at harming or demeaning any group or individual

As with everything I do, this book is for my daughters,
who are the brightest lights in my life. May you enjoy good health
and scary movies for a hundred years with me.

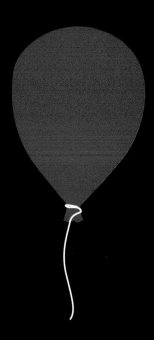

CONTENTS

INTRODUCTION

If you are familiar with my Beetle House restaurants and first cookbook, *Nightmare Before Dinner,* then you know that I love Halloween. So, it was only natural that I went even darker with this cookbook, with recipes inspired by two of my passions: horror movies and healthier eating. In my first cookbook, I included plant-based, or vegan, variations for all the recipes, whereas this one is entirely plant-based.

I didn't set out to write a vegan cookbook, and it isn't about living a vegan lifestyle but about delicious food that you can feel good about eating. I have lived as a strict vegan, but now find myself somewhere in between being a vegetarian and a pescatarian, with a lot of grace and moderation. What I've discovered is that, even if you can't fully commit to a plant-based diet, eating a partial plant-based diet has personal and global benefits.

So, how does the macabre play into this? Well, as evidenced by my restaurants and pop-ups over the years, I enjoy a good theme, and combining horror with plant-based food felt tongue in cheek, in which the only blood found in this book is made from beets. And I, like millions of others, can easily escape into watching hours of horror films. We all have our different reasons for "enjoying" horror. For me, it reminds me of how good things are even when they seem so bad. The fantasy reality of horror will never compare to the reality we live in (hopefully). Imagine never being able to sleep or you'll die, or having a demonic entity trying to kill you over and over and over again. Suddenly, making my rent payment doesn't seem too bad! I have always found horror to be a fun reality check—the attraction to the dark has emphasized the light in my life. It's a classic negative turned into a positive.

I think of plant-based food in the same way. Sure, we can eat raw veggies and fruits all day long, but we are still attracted to the darker side of eating, the triple-stacked burgers and overloaded chili fries. So, I set out to create big, tasty, stick-to-your-ribs comfort foods, inspired by my favorite horror movies and TV shows, that just happen to be plant-based. The mission is to feed you, entertain you, and keep you out of the grave a little longer! Please share with me your thoughts on all things food and horror @therealzachneil and let me know how your dishes turn out. Let's try to keep the horror in the fantasy genre and not a reality for anyone, so please be kind to each other, recognize systems of oppression around you, and do what you can to change them.

IN LOVE, FOOD, AND DARKNESS,
ZACH NEIL

KITCHEN MUST-HAVES

Even the creepiest of kitchens should be well-stocked! Here are some essential tools and ingredients for not only making the frightful food and drink recipes in this book, but also for creating your own smorgasbord of horrors.

TOOLS

Baking sheets
Cocktail shaker
Food processor, blender, and/or immersion blender
Instant Pot (or other pressure-cooking device)
Kitchen torch (optional)
Saucepans (various sizes)

Skillets (various sizes)
Large heavy-bottomed pot
Loaf pan (8½ × 4½ inches, or 22 × 11 cm)
Mixing bowls (various sizes)
Muddler
Smoking gun (optional)
Spoons, spatulas, and whisks
Stand or hand mixer

INGREDIENTS

Agave syrup
All-purpose flour
Apple cider vinegar
Baking powder

Baking soda
Braggs Amino Acids
Coconut cream
Coconut milk

Cornstarch
Liquid smoke
Maple syrup (pure)
Natural food coloring
Nutritional yeast
Oils (olive, coconut, canola, vegetable, avocado, etc.)
Peppercorns (black, white)
Salt (table, kosher, sea)
Soy sauce

Spices (Cajun seasoning, cayenne pepper, celery salt, chili powder, crushed red pepper flakes, dried basil, dried oregano, garlic powder, ground cinnamon, ground cumin, ground mustard, Italian seasoning, onion powder, paprika, smoked paprika)
Sugar (granulated and brown)
Sriracha sauce
Vegetable broth

VEGAN INGREDIENTS

The variety of vegan substitutions available these days for some of our favorite foods is, fortunately, not the stuff of nightmares. These are the "meat" and "dairy" ingredients found in the book along with recommended brands.

Beef, ground and patties (Beyond, Impossible)
Butter (see also the homemade butter recipe on page 127)
Cheese, slices and shreds (Follow Your Heart, Tofutti All American, Chao Creamy
   Original, Violife, Daiya)
Chorizo (Soyrizo)
Cream cheese (Spero Sunflower Cream Cheese, Tofutti Better Than Cream Cheese;
   sometimes I mix brands together to get a deeper texture and taste)
Hot Dogs (Lightlife)
Mayonnaise (Hellmann's)
Sour cream (Tofutti Better Than Sour Cream)
Soy and nut milks (preferably plain and unsweetened, unless otherwise indicated)

SETTING A SCENE

Throughout the book, I share some over-the-top ways to serve the dishes by setting a scene. Just like your favorite '80s horror film, there's no need to be subtle. Even if you aren't already a collector of all things Halloween, Goth, and horror, I'm sure you can find props around the house to enhance a night of dinner, cocktails, and watching your favorite scary movies with friends. It can be as simple as serving everything on black plates in candlelight to going all out with a theme inspired by the movies and TV shows featured in the book and listed below. And if nothing else is coming to mind, a little spatter of blood should do the trick (see Beet Ketchup on page 125).

MOVIES

3 from Hell
Alone in the Dark
American Psycho
Andy Warhol's Blood for Dracula
Bone Tomahawk
Carrie
Child's Play 3
Children of the Corn
The Crow
Dawn of the Dead
Deep Red
Devil's Rejects
Dracula
Drag Me to Hell
The Evil Dead
The Exorcist
Friday the 13th
Halloween
Hannibal
Hannibal Rising
Hellraiser

The Hills Have Eyes
House of 1000 Corpses
It
Killer Klowns from Outer Space
The Lost Boys
The New York Ripper
A Nightmare on Elm Street
Poltergeist
Psycho
Pumpkinhead
Red Dragon
Rosemary's Baby
Scream
The Silence of the Lambs
The Shining
Sleepaway Camp
Sleepy Hollow
The Texas Chainsaw Massacre
Trick 'r Treat
Us

TV SHOWS

American Horror Story: Freak Show
Dexter
Goosebumps
Hannibal

It (miniseries)
True Blood
The Walking Dead

"We all go a little mad sometimes."
Psycho, 1960.

SICKENING STARTERS & SIDES

CRYSTAL LAKE BBQ SLIDERS

INSPIRED BY Friday the 13th

There's nothing better than warm sunshine, a campfire, and working up an appetite after escaping the clutches of Jason Voorhees. These BBQ pulled mushroom sliders are made using an Instant Pot, and the result is bloody delicious!

Yield: 4 to 6 sliders Prep time: 15 minutes Cook time: 45 minutes

DEADLY INGREDIENTS

8 ounces (227 g) portobello mushrooms, sliced

8 ounces (227 g) oyster mushrooms, pulled apart

8 ounces (227 g) shiitake mushrooms, sliced

1½ teaspoons chopped garlic

¼ cup (60 ml) apple cider vinegar

½ teaspoon freshly ground black pepper

1 teaspoon salt

1½ teaspoons liquid smoke

¼ cup (55 g) packed brown sugar

¼ cup (66 g) tomato paste

½ cup (58 g) chopped onion

½ teaspoon cayenne pepper

¾ cup (180 ml) of water

½ cup (120 ml) bourbon

4 to 6 vegan slider buns, for serving

4 to 6 slices vegan cheese of choice, for serving

Wasabi Slaw (page 50), for serving (optional)

1. To an Instant Pot, add the mushrooms, garlic, apple cider vinegar, black pepper, salt, liquid smoke, brown sugar, tomato paste, onion, cayenne, water, and bourbon. Stir to combine.

2. Cook on high pressure for 30 minutes. Allow to cool for 15 minutes after cooking is completed, releasing the pressure manually.

3. To assemble the sliders, top the bottom slider buns with the mushrooms, cheese slices, wasabi slaw (if using), and top buns.

SET THE SCENE

Serve the sliders on a machete! Carefully lay a clean machete on its side, being cautious of the sharp side of the blade so as not to cut yourself. Place the bottom buns in a tight row on the top of the blade, and then top with the mushrooms, cheese slices, wasabi slaw (if using), and top buns. Using the machete as the serving tray, place it in the center of the table for your guests.

KILLER CLOWN CAVIAR

INSPIRED BY Captain Spaulding FROM THE Devil's Rejects, House of 1000 Corpses, AND 3 from Hell

This version of cowboy caviar, infused with Tex-Mex flavors, is as colorful and spicy as Captain Spaulding himself.

Yield: 2 to 4 servings Prep time: 15 minutes (plus 30 minutes marinating time)

DEADLY INGREDIENTS

COWBOY CAVIAR

2 (15-ounce, or 425-g) cans black-eyed peas (or about 3 cups cooked black-eyed peas), drained and rinsed

1 (15-ounce, or 425-g) can black beans (or 1½ cups cooked black beans), drained and rinsed

1 (15.25-ounce, or 432-g) can whole kernel corn (or 1½ cups frozen corn, thawed), drained and rinsed

1 red bell pepper, finely chopped

1 cup (150 g) chopped cherry tomatoes

½ cup (50 g) finely chopped scallions

¼ cup (34 g) finely chopped sweet pickled jalapeño peppers

¼ cup (35 g) chopped roasted red peppers

½ teaspoon chili powder

SAUCE

2 teaspoons kosher salt

¼ cup (60 ml) apple cider vinegar

2½ tablespoons sugar

½ teaspoon garlic powder

½ teaspoon ground cumin

¼ cup (60 ml) olive oil

3 tablespoons lime juice

¼ teaspoon Tabasco

1 teaspoon dried basil

SERVING

Blue and red organic tortilla chips (circus colors)

1. To make the cowboy caviar: To a large bowl, add the beans, corn, bell pepper, cherry tomatoes, scallions, jalapeños, roasted red peppers, and chili powder. Set aside.

2. To make the sauce: In a medium bowl, mix together the salt, apple cider vinegar, sugar, garlic powder, cumin, olive oil, lime juice, Tabasco, and basil.

SET THE SCENE

Serve this dish with your best killer-clown props: wigs, clown noses, even a bloody playing board with clown gloves. Use your imagination to bring this Texan snack to life—or death. Eat while watching the Captain Spaulding movies and enjoy!

3. Pour the sauce over the beans and veggies and mix well. Cover and marinate in the refrigerator for 30 to 45 minutes.

4. Serve in the bowl of your choosing with the colorful tortilla chips.

5. Leftovers can be refrigerated in an airtight container for up to 2 weeks.

DEVIL'S NIGHT CAULIFLOWER WINGS

INSPIRED BY The Crow

Although *The Crow* is not considered a horror film, its portrayal of Devil's Night, a night of mayhem that takes place just before Halloween, inspired this dish that will set the mood for any evening of watching horror movies.

Yield: 2 to 4 servings **Prep time: 15 minutes** **Cook time: 35 minutes**

DEADLY INGREDIENTS

CAULIFLOWER WINGS
1 medium to large head cauliflower

2 cups (240 g) all-purpose flour, divided

½ teaspoon white pepper

½ teaspoon onion powder

1 tablespoon garlic powder

1 teaspoon smoked paprika

⅓ cup (40 g) cornstarch

1½ teaspoons kosher salt

2 cups (475 ml) club soda

SAUCE
¼ cup (60 ml) Chainsaw Hot Sauce (page 123) or Buffalo-style hot sauce of choice

¼ cup (60 ml) Vegan Butter (page 127) or vegan butter of choice, melted

2 teaspoons white vinegar

¼ teaspoon garlic powder

½ teaspoon onion powder

2½ teaspoons sugar

SERVING
Tex-Mex Ranch (page 124), for dipping (optional)

1. Preheat the oven to 425°F (220°C; gas mark 7). Line two baking sheets with parchment paper or foil and place a baking rack on top of each one. Set aside.

2. To make the cauliflower wings: Cut the cauliflower into bite-size pieces.

3. In a medium bowl, mix 1 cup (120 g) of the flour with the white pepper, ½ teaspoon onion powder, 1 tablespoon garlic powder, smoked paprika, cornstarch, and salt. Pour in the club soda and stir until a batter forms.

SET THE SCENE
Plate the cauliflower wings on a black surface so that the red and orange colors pop. Serve pitchfork cocktail picks.

4. Add the remaining 1 cup (120 g) flour to a medium bowl.

5. Coat each cauliflower piece in the flour, then dip it into the batter. Place the pieces on top of the prepared racks (the batter will drip below).

6. Put the baking sheets with the racks in the oven and bake for 15 minutes, then rotate the sheets and bake for 12 more minutes, until crispy.

7. While the cauliflower wings bake, make the sauce: In a small bowl, mix together the hot sauce, melted butter, ¼ teaspoon garlic powder, ½ teaspoon onion powder, and sugar.

8. Let the cauliflower wings cool for 5 to 7 minutes. Use tongs to transfer them to a large bowl. Pour the sauce over the wings and mix until well coated.

9. Serve immediately with the Tex-Mex ranch (if using).

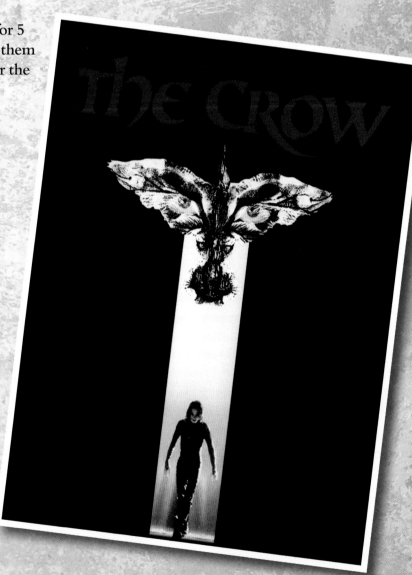

CHARCOAL ARUGULA SALAD

INSPIRED BY American Psycho

Patrick Bateman thinks that this menu item at Texarkana is "outrageous," and so will you—in a good way of course. Enjoy it like the true psycho you are!

Yield: 2 to 4 servings Prep time: 20 minutes

DEADLY INGREDIENTS

ARUGULA SALAD
4 cups (80 g) arugula

¼ cup (29 g) chopped red onion

¼ cup (33 g) chopped cucumber

¼ cup (45 g) chopped black olives

¼ cup (28 g) chopped walnuts

¼ cup (45 g) chopped tomato

¼ cup 935 g) chopped roasted red peppers

¼ cup (30 g) thinly sliced radish

¼ cup (38 g) fresh blueberries

¼ teaspoon kosher salt, for garnishing

¼ teaspoon smoked paprika, for garnishing

CHARCOAL DRESSING
¼ cup (30 g) Tex-Mex Ranch (page 124)

1 tablespoon liquid-activated coconut charcoal

1. To make the arugula salad: In a large bowl, combine the arugula, onion, cucumber, olives, walnuts, tomato, red peppers, radish, and blueberries. Toss well and set aside.

2. To make the charcoal dressing: In a small bowl, stir together the ranch and coconut charcoal.

3. To serve, divide the salad among salad plates, add a dollop of the charcoal dressing on top, and then sprinkle with the salt and smoked paprika.

NOTE

You can buy liquid-activated coconut charcoal online and at stores that sell nutritional supplements.

THE HILLS HAVE FRIES

INSPIRED BY The Hills Have Eyes

All eyes will be on you while you eat this hill of loaded hand-cut french fries.

Yield: 3 servings Prep time: 20 minutes (plus overnight soaking time)
Cook time: 1 hour

DEADLY INGREDIENTS

FRENCH FRIES
4 medium russet potatoes

3 quarts (2.8 L) oil, for frying

Salt and freshly ground black pepper, to taste

BÉCHAMEL
4 cups (950 ml) unsweetened almond milk

1 cup (240 ml) soy creamer (such as Silk brand)

2 tablespoons soy sauce

2 tablespoons nutritional yeast

¼ cup (60 g) vegan cream cheese

6 slices vegan cheese

4 cups (480 g) shredded vegan cheddar cheese

4 cups (480 g) shredded vegan Monterey or pepper jack cheese

8 slices vegan American cheese

2 teaspoons yellow mustard

1 teaspoon salt

3 tablespoons cornstarch

CHILI SAUCE
3 tablespoons oil

3 tablespoons oil

1 large onion, chopped

3 cloves garlic, minced

1 package vegan ground beef

2 tablespoons yellow mustard

4 tablespoons chili powder

1 teaspoon ground cumin

½ teaspoon cayenne pepper

1 teaspoon vegan Worcestershire sauce

2 teaspoons garlic powder

1 teaspoon onion powder

1 teaspoon crushed red pepper flakes

1 cup (130 g) vegan refried beans

1 recipe Blood and Basil Sauce (page 131) or 1 (16-ounce, or 454-g) jar marinara sauce of choice

1 tablespoon apple cider vinegar

CILANTRO AND LIME SOUR CREAM
Salt and freshly ground pepper, to taste

1 cup (240 g) vegan sour cream

1 tablespoon fresh squeezed lime juice

1 tablespoon finely chopped fresh cilantro

Salt, to taste

TOPPINGS
3 strips vegan bacon

4 scallions, thinly sliced

½ red onion, finely chopped

Fresh cilantro leaves (optional)

THE LUCKY ONES DIED FIRST!

1. **To make the french fries (for a baked option, see tip):** Slice the potatoes ½ inch (1 cm) thick, or use a french fry dye press if you have one. Soak them in cold water, cover, and refrigerate overnight.

2. Rinse the fries twice in cold water, then pat them dry completely.

3. In a large heavy-bottomed pot or deep fryer, heat the 3 quarts (2.8 L) oil to 300°F (150°C). Line a baking sheet with parchment paper and set aside.

4. Add the fries in handfuls to the oil, being careful not to overcrowd the fry basket, and cook for 5 to 6 minutes, until golden brown. Transfer the fries to the prepared baking sheet and freeze them before frying them a second time. Meanwhile, make the sauces and toppings.

(continued on page 26)

(continued from page 25)

5. To make the béchamel: In a large saucepan, heat the milk, creamer, and soy creamer over medium heat until thick. Slowly whisk in the nutritional yeast, cream cheese, and sliced and shredded cheeses, allowing the cheeses to melt. Add the 2 teaspoons mustard, 1 teaspoon salt, and cornstarch. Whisk for 5 minutes, or until thick.

6. To make the chili sauce: In a medium saucepan, heat the 3 tablespoons oil over medium heat. Add the garlic and onion and cook for 3 to 5 minutes, until the onion is almost translucent.

7. Add the ground beef, mustard, chili powder, cumin, cayenne, Worcestershire, garlic powder, onion powder, and red pepper flakes. Cook the meat until done according to the package instructions.

8. Add the refried beans, tomato sauce, and vinegar and cook until the mixture reaches a chili sauce consistency.

9. To make the cilantro and lime sour cream: In a large bowl, whip together the sour cream, lime juice, and chopped cilantro. Season with salt.

10. To make the toppings: Cook the bacon according to the package instructions, then chop it into bits.

11. When ready to fry for the second time, heat the oil to 375°F (190°C). Line a tray with paper towels.

12. Fry the frozen fries in handful-size batches until golden brown, about 5 minutes. Transfer the fries to the prepared tray to drain and season with salt and pepper immediately.

13. To assemble, in a large bowl, drench the fries in the béchamel sauce, then transfer to a serving platter. Cover the fries with the chili sauce; add a dollop of the cilantro and lime sour cream; sprinkle with the scallions, bacon, and red onions; and top with the cilantro (if using).

NOTE

For baked fries, soak the cut potatoes in cold water for 45 minutes, then dry them extremely well, dabbing them with a towel or putting them through a salad spinner. Line a baking sheet with parchment paper. Toss the fries in ¼ cup (60 ml) canola or olive oil and spread them in a single layer on the baking sheet. Bake at 375°F (190°C; gas mark 5) for 15 to 20 minutes, until golden brown, then turn up the heat to 425°F (220°C; gas mark 7) to really crisp them up, for about 20 minutes.

❧ BUFFALO FRIES ❧

INSPIRED BY Comfort Horror

Oddly enough, a lot of people find watching horror films comforting. So why not pair watching your favorite scary movie with some comfort food? These spicy, tangy fries should do the trick.

Yield: 4 to 6 servings Prep time: 5 minutes Cook time: 35 minutes

DEADLY INGREDIENTS

16 to 24 ounces (454 to 680 g) frozen french fries

Oil, for coating

1 tablespoon Cajun seasoning

½ teaspoon celery salt

½ cup (120 g) buffalo sauce

½ cup (120 g) Tex-Mex Ranch (page 124)

I. Preheat the oven to 400°F (205°C; gas mark 6).

2. Place the fries on a baking sheet. Coat them with a tiny amount of oil, then sprinkle with the Cajun seasoning and celery salt.

3. Bake for 35 to 45 minutes, until golden brown.

4. In a large bowl, toss the fries with the buffalo sauce until lightly and evenly coated but not soggy.

5. Serve with the Tex-Mex ranch as a dipping sauce.

NOTE

If you prefer to make hand-cut french fries, follow steps 1 to 4 and 11 to 12 in The Hills Have Fries on page 24.

ICHABOD'S BREAD

INSPIRED BY Sleepy Hollow

You'll want to hold onto your head to enjoy the fall flavors found in this bread.

Yield: 8 servings Prep time: 20 minutes Cook time: 40 minutes

DEADLY INGREDIENTS

2 tablespoons ground flaxseed

⅓ cup (80 ml) water

1 cup (240 ml) unsweetened creamy vanilla cashew milk (such as Silk)

1 tablespoon apple cider vinegar

2¼ cups (270 g) all-purpose flour

1 cup (220 g) packed light brown sugar

2½ teaspoons pumpkin pie spice

1 teaspoon baking soda

1 teaspoon baking powder

1 teaspoon salt

⅓ cup (80 ml) coconut oil (or canola oil)

1 cup (120 g) dried cranberries

1 cup (112 g) chopped walnuts

Vegan Butter (page 127) or vegan butter of choice, softened, for serving

1. Preheat the oven to 350°F (175°C; gas mark 4). Grease an 8½ × 4½-inch (22 × 11 cm) loaf pan and set aside.

2. In a small bowl, combine the flaxseed and water (this is your egg replacement) and whisk well. Set aside. (It will thicken a little while sitting.)

3. In a separate small bowl, mix together the cashew milk and apple cider vinegar to create a vegan buttermilk.

4. In a large bowl, whisk together the flour, brown sugar, pumpkin pie spice, baking soda, baking powder, and salt.

5. In a separate large bowl, whisk together the coconut oil with the vegan buttermilk and flax mixture.

6. Add the egg replacement and buttermilk to the dry ingredients and whisk until well blended. Whisk in the dried cranberries and walnuts, then pour the batter into the prepared pan.

7. Bake for 40 to 60 minutes, until a toothpick inserted into the center comes out clean. If the top browns before the bread is done, cover with foil.

8. Remove from the oven and allow to cool before slicing and slathering with the softened vegan butter.

 HERBED BREAD

INSPIRED BY **Rosemary's Baby**

This bread only has hints of rosemary and sage, not tannis root. A warm, fresh loaf will surely please those nosy, seemingly harmless neighbors . . .

Yield: 4 to 6 servings **Prep time:** 20 minutes (plus 1 hour 15 minutes rising time) **Cook time:** 35 minutes

DEADLY INGREDIENTS

2½ cups (595 ml) warm water, divided, plus more if needed

2½ teaspoons active dry yeast

½ teaspoon granulated sugar

5 cups (600 g) bread flour, plus more if needed

¼ cup (55 g) packed brown sugar

1½ teaspoons salt

3 tablespoons olive oil, plus more for coating and if needed

½ cup (12 g) chopped fresh sage

½ cup (14 g) chopped fresh rosemary

1 cup (115 g) chopped red onion

1. Pour ¼ cup (60 ml) of the warm water into the bowl of a stand mixer, then add the yeast and granulated sugar. Set aside for 8 to 10 minutes, or until the yeast has bubbled up.

2. Add the flour, brown sugar, and salt to the bowl with the yeast mixture. Stir to combine. Add the remaining 2¼ cups (535 ml) warm water, olive oil, herbs, and onion. Using the dough hook attachment, mix on low speed for 5 to 7 minutes, until the dough has formed a smooth ball. If the dough is too dry, add a little more olive oil or water, and if too wet, add a little more flour.

3. Coat the dough lightly with olive oil and transfer to a large bowl. Cover the bowl with a damp cloth or floured plastic wrap and place in a warm spot to rise for 45 to 60 minutes, or until the dough is doubled in size.

4. Punch the dough down and knead it a little to get the air out. Shape the dough like a torpedo, put it on a baking sheet, and cover with a damp rag or greased plastic wrap to proof again. Let it rise for about 30 minutes.

5. Meanwhile, preheat the oven to 450°F (230°C; gas mark 8).

6. Reshape the dough as needed to a ball shape and, using a peel or your hands, transfer it to a baking stone (preferred) or a baking sheet to bake for 35 to 45 minutes, or until dark brown. (When the bread is done, it should sound hollow when you knock on it.)

EVIL BREAD

INSPIRED BY The Evil Dead

It's quite okay to read from this book aloud. This recipe will only possess you with the desire to never eat basic corn bread again.

Yield: 8 servings **Prep time: 15 minutes** **Cook time: 25 minutes**

DEADLY INGREDIENTS

1¼ cups (150 g) all-purpose flour

1 cup (140 g) yellow cornmeal

⅔ cup (135 g) sugar

1 teaspoon salt

1 tablespoon baking powder

1¼ cups (295 ml) unsweetened almond milk

⅓ cup (80 ml) canola oil

1 cup (164 g) drained canned corn

½ cup (68 g) finely chopped pickled jalapeños

½ cup (58 g) finely chopped red onion

½ cup (35 g) finely chopped roasted red peppers

1. Preheat the oven to 400°F (205°C; gas mark 6). Grease an 8 × 8-inch (20 × 20 cm) square pan or an 8-inch (20 cm) round cake pan and set aside.

2. In a large bowl, whisk together the flour, cornmeal, sugar, salt, and baking powder.

3. Add the almond milk, canola oil, corn, jalapeños, onion, and red peppers. Mix well.

4. Transfer the batter to the prepared pan, and bake for 20 to 25 minutes, or until a toothpick inserted into the center comes out clean. Serve at room temperature.

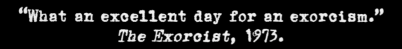
"What an excellent day for an exorcism."
The Exorcist, 1973.

MONSTROUS
MAINS

FRED'S BURGER

INSPIRED BY A Nightmare on Elm Street

This sandwich picks up the look and feel of the classic overstuffed burger of the 1980s with its nacho cheese sauce, sweet onion jam, and a little heat. Enjoy it while hanging out and watching *Nightmare* or any other of your favorite '80s horror movies.

Yield: 1 sandwich **Prep time:** 10 minutes **Cook time:** 15 minutes

DEADLY INGREDIENTS

1 tablespoon olive oil

1 vegan burger patty

Vamp Paste (page 128), to taste

1 vegan hamburger bun

2 slices vegan pepper jack cheese

1 piece romaine lettuce

1 slice tomato

1 tablespoon Totally '80s Cheese Sauce (page 129)

1 tablespoon Sweet Onion Jam (page 130)

1 tablespoon Chainsaw BBQ Sauce (page 122) or BBQ sauce of choice

1 tablespoon minced roasted red peppers

1 smoking gun (or your favorite instant food-smoking device) (see Note below)

1. Cook the burger patty according to the package instructions. Remove the burger patty from the pan and set aside.

2. Spread the vamp paste on the inside of both halves of the hamburger bun. Heat a small skillet over medium heat and toast the bun, cut sides down, until the insides are golden brown, about 2 to 3 minutes. Transfer the bun to a plate.

3. To assemble, place the burger patty on the bottom bun and top with the sliced pepper jack. Add these ingredients in this order: lettuce, tomato, cheese sauce, onion jam, and roasted red peppers. Spread the barbecue sauce on the inside of the top bun. Add the top bun.

4. Place the entire burger in a plastic bag or another container, insert the tube of the smoking gun, close the container, and push smoke inside the bag or container for 1 minute.

5. Serve with your favorite props (Freddy glove, fake blood—wherever your morbid imagination takes you)!

NOTE

A smoking gun is a quick and easy way to add smoky flavors to food and drinks. You can purchase a smoking gun or a similar tool online. Follow the instructions that come with the smoking gun to use.

OUIJA BOARD PEA SOUP

INSPIRED BY The Exorcist

This split pea soup, made in an Instant Pot, is warm, cozy, and perfect for a crisp fall evening watching *The Exorcist*. Let's hope you can keep it down . . .

Yield: 2 to 4 servings **Prep time: 15 minutes** **Cook time: 25 minutes**

DEADLY INGREDIENTS

6 cups (1.4 L) water

1 teaspoon Better Than Bouillon Sautéed Onion Base

1 teaspoon Better Than Bouillon Seasoned Vegetable Base

1 cup (130 g) chopped rainbow carrots

3 stalks celery, chopped

¼ cup (6 g) chopped fresh sage

1 teaspoon dried thyme

1 tablespoon minced garlic

¼ cup (10 g) finely chopped chives

2 cups (395 g) dried green split peas, rinsed

1 cup (150 g) chopped red potatoes

1 teaspoon liquid smoke

1 tablespoon agave syrup

½ teaspoon white pepper

Salt, to taste

Slices of Herbed Bread (page 31) or bread of choice, for serving (optional)

1. In a medium bowl, mix together the water and onion and vegetable bouillon bases well.

2. To an Instant Pot, add the bouillon mixture and the carrots, celery, sage, thyme, garlic, chives, green split peas, potatoes, liquid smoke, agave, and white pepper. Stir to combine.

3. Cook on high pressure and heat for 20 minutes (the Bean/Chili setting), releasing the pressure manually.

4. Stir well and season with salt.

5. Ladle the hot soup into bowls and serve with bread slices (if using).

SET THE SCENE

Serve the soup bowls on top of a Ouija board with a rosary and bread slices shaped into planchettes.

DRAG ME TO BELL

INSPIRED BY Drag Me to Hell

Hot as hell but sinfully blissful, these stuffed bell peppers, relleno-style, will make you want to crawl back for more.

Yield: 4 servings Prep time: 20 minutes Cook time: 1 hour

DEADLY INGREDIENTS

SAFFRON RICE

1½ cups (285 g) long-grain white rice

3 cups (700 ml) vegetable broth

1 teaspoon Mexican saffron threads (or regular saffron threads)

½ teaspoon turmeric

MEAT

1 package vegan ground beef

1 cup (128 g) soy chorizo (such as Soyrizo), casing removed and crumbled

2 teaspoons chili powder

Salt, to taste

CHILI LIME AIOLI

2 cups (448 g) vegan mayonnaise

Juice from 2 limes

½ teaspoon salt

1 teaspoon chili powder

2 tablespoons adobo sauce (from a can of chipotle peppers in adobo sauce)

MINI BELL PEPPERS

24 sweet mini bell peppers, stems and seeds removed

Oil, for coating

Pinch salt

VEGETABLES

1 carrot

1 tablespoon oil

½ red onion, quartered

1 jalapeño pepper

Salt and freshly ground black pepper, to taste

1 tablespoon canned chipotle peppers in adobo sauce

FRY BATTER

1½ cups (360 ml) unsweetened almond milk

1½ tablespoons apple cider vinegar

½ cup (60 g) cornstarch

2 cups (240 g) all-purpose flour

2 tablespoons chili powder

2 teaspoons salt

4 cups (600 g) panko bread crumbs

Oil, for frying

SERVING

4 tablespoons fresh micro cilantro

1. To make the saffron rice: In a large saucepan, combine the rice, broth, and saffron threads. Cover and heat until boiling. Reduce the heat to a simmer. After 10 to 12 minutes, when small holes form in the rice, remove the pan from the heat and let the rice continue to absorb the remaining liquid, 5 to 10 more minutes. Set aside.

2. To make the meat: In a large skillet, combine the ground beef, soy chorizo, and chili powder over medium heat and cook until the meat is cooked through. Season with salt. Set aside.

3. To make the chili lime aioli: In a small bowl, whisk together the mayonnaise, lime juice, ½ teaspoon salt, 1 teaspoon chili powder, and adobo sauce thoroughly. Set aside. (Refrigerate any extra in an airtight container for up to 10 days.)

4. To make the mini bell peppers: Preheat the oven to 400°F (205°C; gas mark 6). Line a baking sheet with parchment paper.

5. Lightly coat the peppers with oil and season with the pinch of salt. Place on the prepared baking sheet. Bake for 3 to 5 minutes, until slightly tender. Allow the peppers to cool in the refrigerator.

6. To make the vegetables: Cut the sides of the carrot to square it off, then thinly slice it crosswise.

7. In a medium skillet, heat the 1 tablespoon oil over medium heat. Add the carrots, onions, jalapeño, salt, and pepper and cook until the vegetables are tender and have a slight char to them. Let the vegetables cool, then roughly chop them into small pieces. In a small bowl, mix the vegetables with the chipotle peppers in adobo sauce. Set aside.

8. To make the fry batter: In a small bowl, mix together the almond milk and apple cider vinegar to create a vegan buttermilk.

9. In a separate small bowl, mix together the cornstarch, flour, chili powder, and salt. Divide this mixture between two medium bowls, adding the panko to one of the bowls. You should have three bowls: one dry mix without panko, one dry mix with panko, and the vegan buttermilk.

10. In a large bowl, mix together the saffron rice, meat, and vegetables for the filling.

11. To assemble, stuff the filling into the mini bell peppers with a spoon and fill all the way to the top. Dust the stuffed peppers in the dry mix without panko, then dip them in the vegan buttermilk, and then dust them in the dry mix with panko.

12. Heat 1½ inches (4 cm) of oil in a large heavy-bottomed pot to 350°F (175°C). Working in batches, deep-fry the stuffed peppers for 3 minutes, or until golden brown.

13. Serve 6 stuffed peppers per plate with the chili lime aioli. Garnish each plate with 1 tablespoon of micro cilantro.

TEXAS BBQ CHIKON BURGER

INSPIRED BY The Texas Chainsaw Massacre

These make-'em-yourself vegan chicken burgers have the perfect Southern kick, and even those with a cannibalistic appetite won't be able to resist them. The burgers are also great for chicken sandwiches, chicken Parmesan, and even chopped up in salads.

Yield: 5 sandwiches Prep time: 20 minutes Cook time: 1 hour

DEADLY INGREDIENTS

CHIKON BURGERS
Vegetable oil, for greasing the sheet pan

1 (15-ounce, or 425-g) can chickpeas, drained and rinsed

½ cup (68 g) cooked brown rice

¼ cup plus 2½ tablespoons olive oil, divided

2 tablespoons water, plus more if needed

¾ cup (45 g) panko bread crumbs (or gluten-free bread crumbs)

¼ cup (34 g) finely chopped roasted red peppers

⅓ cup (33 g) chopped scallions

¼ cup (28 g) shredded carrots

½ cup (35 g) chopped mushrooms of choice

1½ tablespoons nutritional yeast

1½ teaspoons salt

2 teaspoons brown sugar

1 teaspoon garlic powder

½ teaspoon paprika

½ teaspoon smoked paprika

½ teaspoon chili powder

½ teaspoon ground mustard

¼ teaspoon cayenne pepper

¼ cup (30 g) flour (or gluten-free alternative), plus more if needed

SANDWICH
Vamp Paste (page 128), to taste

5 large vegan hamburger buns

2 tablespoons Chainsaw Hot Sauce (page 123) or hot sauce of choice, divided, plus more if needed

2 tablespoons Chainsaw BBQ Sauce (page 122) or BBQ sauce of choice, divided, plus more if needed

5 slices vegan American or cheddar cheese

5 large leaves romaine lettuce

5 thick slices tomato

15 to 20 pickled jalapeño slices

15 bread-and-butter pickle slices

¼ cup (14 g) crispy french-fried onions (such as Full Circle Market Organic French Fried Onions)

Tex-Mex Ranch (page 124), to taste

1. To make the chikon burgers: Preheat the oven to 375°F (190°C; gas mark 5). Grease a large baking sheet with vegetable oil and set aside.

2. In a medium bowl, mash the chickpeas until they form a paste.

3. Using an immersion blender and a separate bowl or a food processor, blend the cooked brown rice until it is close to a paste consistency. Add the blended rice to the chickpeas and mix well.

4. Add 2½ tablespoons of the olive oil, water, panko, roasted red peppers, scallions, carrots, mushrooms, nutritional yeast, salt, brown sugar, garlic powder, paprika, smoked paprika, chili powder, ground mustard, and cayenne to the chickpea mixture. Mix well.

(continued on page 44)

(continued from page 43)

5. Pour the flour evenly over the top of the mixture and then mix again.

6. Using your hands, knead the mixture like dough for a couple of minutes until it starts to bind together, adding more flour if too thin or more water if too thick. Divide the mixture into 5 equal pieces and form into patties. (The patties can be refrigerated for up to 1 week or frozen for up to 6 months.)

7. Heat the remaining ¼ cup (60 ml) olive oil in a large skillet over medium-low heat. Add the patties to the pan and cook for 2 to 3 minutes per side, until medium golden brown on both sides.

8. Transfer the patties to the prepared baking sheet and bake for 25 to 30 minutes, flipping every 10 minutes to ensure a crispy crust on both sides.

9. To assemble, brush a liberal amount of vamp paste on the insides of both halves of the hamburger buns. Heat a large skillet over medium heat and toast the buns, cut sides down, until the insides are golden brown, about 2 to 3 minutes. Transfer the buns to plates.

10. In a small bowl, mix the hot sauce with the barbecue sauce. Spread 2 teaspoons of the sauce mixture over both sides of each of the "chikon" patties, adding more sauce if needed. This is easy to do in a skillet over low heat, turning the patties in the sauce.

11. Once the patties are well coated, place them on the buns. Make sure the patties are hot enough to melt the cheese, then top each patty with a cheese slice, a piece of romaine lettuce, a tomato slice, and 3 or 4 jalapeño slices. Add a few pickle slices, then top the sandwich with the crispy french-fried onions.

12. Drizzle the sandwiches with a liberal amount of Tex-Mex ranch, then spread about ½ teaspoon more of the barbecue–hot sauce mixture on the inside of each of the top buns.

13. Place the top buns and press the sandwiches down a little to seal it all together.

SET THE SCENE

Buy cheap chainsaw blades at the hardware store, wash and dry them, and place them on the plates. If you have a chainsaw, place it in the center of the table. Drizzle the blades and chains with a little bit of Beet Ketchup (page 125). Place a sandwich on the middle of each blade. Watch *The Texas Chainsaw Massacre* or any of your favorite horror films while eating!

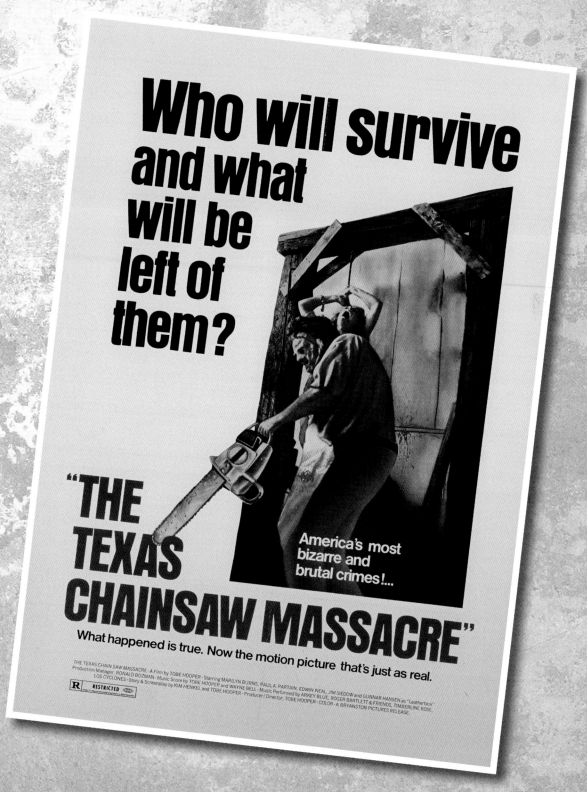

FLESH AND BLOOD

INSPIRED BY Carrie

No one's going to laugh at you after they taste this twist on the classic combo of grilled cheese and tomato soup. The tomato soup is made using an Instant Pot for an extra rich flavor.

Yield: 2 to 4 servings Prep time: 10 minutes Cook time: 20 minutes

DEADLY INGREDIENTS

BLOOD BUCKET SOUP

2 (13.5-ounce, or 400-ml) cans unsweetened coconut cream

2 (14.5-ounce, or 411-g) cans stewed tomatoes

1 (28-ounce, or 794-g) can tomato puree

¾ cup (180 ml) water (swish it around the empty tomato puree can to rinse out the remaining puree, then add to the pot)

¼ teaspoon celery salt

Pinch cayenne pepper (to your heat preference)

½ teaspoon California lemon peel (or 1 tablespoon lemon zest)

¼ teaspoon smoked paprika

1 teaspoon crushed dried rosemary

¼ teaspoon white pepper

⅛ teaspoon garlic powder

3 teaspoons agave syrup

3 tablespoons Bragg Liquid Aminos or soy sauce

6–8 drops natural red food coloring

NAAN FLESH GRILLED CHEESE

2 vegan naans

1 teaspoon Vamp Paste (page 128)

2 slices vegan cheddar cheese

2 slices vegan pepper jack cheese

1. To make the blood bucket soup: To an Instant Pot, add the coconut cream, stewed tomatoes, tomato puree, water, celery salt, cayenne, lemon peel, smoked paprika, rosemary, white pepper, garlic powder, agave, and liquid aminos. Stir together well, breaking up the tomatoes as much as possible.

2. Cook on the Soup/Broth setting, releasing any pressure manually.

3. When finished, stir in the food coloring until you achieve a very bloody color. Add ¾ cup (180 ml) additional water if needed to thin.

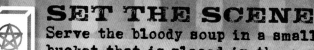

SET THE SCENE

Serve the bloody soup in a small, new, and clean metal bucket that is placed in the center of the table on a circular serving plate. Arrange the grilled-cheese quarters on the plate around the bucket.

4. To make the naan flesh grilled cheese: Coat the outsides of the naan with the vamp paste. Place the cheese on the bread and press the naan together.

5. Grill in a medium skillet over medium-low heat for 2 minutes per side, or until the bread is toasted and golden and the cheese is melting slightly. Remove from the heat, allow to cool for a few minutes, and then cut into quarters.

6. Ladle the hot soup into bowls and serve with the grilled cheese.

⊱ HANNIBAL'S FEAST ⊰

INSPIRED BY Hannibal Lecter

Liver and fava beans may have been Hannibal Lecter's go-to, but this plant-based feast of roasted zucchini topped with cashew ricotta and marinated mushrooms and served with roasted pepper bruschetta on garlic toast should get your lips smacking. Serve with your favorite bottle of Chianti.

Yield: 2 to 4 servings Prep time: 45 minutes (plus 2 hours marinating time)
Cook time: 30 minutes

DEADLY INGREDIENTS

MARINATED MUSHROOMS
1 (3.5-ounce, or 99-g) package whole shiitake mushrooms, stemmed

1 (3.5-ounce, or 99-g) package whole oyster mushrooms

3 tablespoons soy sauce

3 tablespoons olive oil

½ teaspoon garlic powder

1 teaspoon agave syrup

2 tablespoons chopped fresh sage

1 tablespoon finely chopped fresh rosemary

2 tablespoons white wine

ROASTED ZUCCHINI
1 large zucchini

2 tablespoons olive oil

1 teaspoon Italian seasoning

½ teaspoon sea salt

CASHEW RICOTTA
1¼ cups (150 g) roasted salted cashews, soaked in hot water for 30 minutes

1½ tablespoons lemon juice

1½ tablespoons nutritional yeast

½ teaspoon garlic powder

½ teaspoon sea salt

¼ cup (60 ml) water

¼ teaspoon white pepper

½ teaspoon agave syrup

RED PEPPER BRUSCHETTA AND TOAST POINTS
1 cup (260 g) chopped roasted red peppers

½ teaspoon chopped garlic

½ teaspoon sea salt

¼ cup (40 g) chopped red onion

¼ cup (60 ml) olive oil

2 tablespoons balsamic vinegar

1 tablespoon agave syrup

2 slices bread of choice

Vamp Paste (page 128), to taste

1. To make the marinated mushrooms: In a large bowl, combine the whole mushrooms with the soy sauce, 3 tablespoons olive oil, ½ teaspoon garlic powder, 1 teaspoon agave, sage, rosemary, and white wine. Stir together well. Cover the mushrooms and marinate in the refrigerator for at least 2 hours. (Meanwhile, make the other recipe components.)

2. To roast the zucchini: Preheat the oven to 375°F (190°C; gas mark 5).

3. Cut the zucchini into 1-inch-thick (2.5 cm) vertical slices for 4 zucchini fillets. Coat the fillets on both sides with the 2 tablespoons olive oil, Italian seasoning, and ½ teaspoon sea salt.

4. Roast for 20 to 30 minutes, until tender enough to pierce with a fork.

5. To make the cashew ricotta: Combine the soaked cashews, lemon juice, nutritional yeast, ½ teaspoon garlic powder, ½ teaspoon sea salt, water, white pepper, and ½ teaspoon agave in a food processor. Process until smooth and creamy, transfer to a bowl, and set aside.

6. To make the red pepper bruschetta and toast points: Clean the food processor, then add the red peppers, garlic, salt, red onion, ¼ cup (60 ml) olive oil, balsamic vinegar, and 1 tablespoon agave to it. Pulse 5 to 7 times to chop. Transfer the bruschetta to an airtight container and refrigerate for up to 1 month.

7. Cut the crusts off the bread slices and discard. Toast the slices, spread with vamp paste, and then cut each slice diagonally into 4 triangles for toast points.

8. After the mushrooms are marinated, stir the mushrooms and marinade together to recombine, then add the mushrooms and marinade to a large saucepan. Cover and heat on low to medium for 7 to 10 minutes, stirring occasionally, until the mushrooms are cooked through and soft.

9. Place 2 zucchini fillets on each plate, spread a liberal amount of the cashew ricotta on them, top with the marinated mushrooms, and drizzle some of the marinated mushroom sauce over the top of them.

10. Spread the red pepper bruschetta on the toast points and place 2 on each plate.

WHO'S FOR DINNER?

INSPIRED BY Hannibal Lecter

"I do wish we could chat longer, but I'm having an old friend for dinner." Fortunately, this braised tofu topped with sautéed mushrooms and scallions and served with wasabi slaw, spicy mayo, and sesame garlic bok choy is plant-based. Serve with a nice sake.

Yield: 2 to 4 servings Prep time: 20 minutes Cook time: 25 minutes

DEADLY INGREDIENTS

WASABI SLAW

1 teaspoon powdered wasabi

½ teaspoon sesame oil

½ teaspoon sea salt

¼ cup (60 ml) apple cider vinegar

1½ tablespoons agave syrup

4 cups (340 g) shredded (or thinly sliced) red cabbage

SAUTÉED MUSHROOMS AND SCALLIONS

1 teaspoon olive oil

8 ounces (227 g) mixed oyster and shiitake mushrooms

½ cup (50 g) finely chopped scallions

2 teaspoons less-sodium soy sauce

½ teaspoon minced fresh ginger

1 teaspoon agave syrup

SPICY MAYO

1½ tablespoons vegan mayonnaise

¼ teaspoon agave syrup

¼ teaspoon sriracha sauce

BRAISED TOFU

¼ cup (60 ml) vegetable or olive oil, plus more if needed

8 ounces (227 g) firm or extra-firm tofu

¼ cup (60 ml) less-sodium soy sauce

¼ cup (55 g) packed light brown sugar

1 teaspoon minced garlic

¼ teaspoon sesame oil

¼ teaspoon gochujang

1 teaspoon lemon juice

½ teaspoon agave syrup

¼ cup (60 ml) water

SESAME GARLIC BOK CHOY

1 teaspoon minced garlic

2 teaspoons less-sodium soy sauce

1 teaspoon agave syrup

1 teaspoon lemon juice

½ teaspoon olive oil

¼ teaspoon sesame oil

1. To make the wasabi slaw: In a medium bowl, mix together the wasabi, ½ teaspoon sesame oil, sea salt, apple cider vinegar, 1½ tablespoons agave, and cabbage until well combined. Cover and let sit in the refrigerator for 30 to 45 minutes before serving.

2. To make the sautéed mushrooms: In a large skillet, heat the 1 teaspoon olive oil over medium heat. Add the mushrooms, scallions, 2 teaspoons soy sauce, and ginger and cook until the mushrooms are soft, about 5 minutes. Add the 1 teaspoon agave during the last minute of cooking. Remove from the heat and set aside.

3. To make the spicy mayo: In a small bowl, mix together the mayonnaise, ¼ teaspoon agave, and sriracha until well combined. Set aside.

4. To make the braised tofu: In a large skillet, heat the vegetable oil over medium heat. Slice the tofu into 1-inch (2.5 cm) cubes, then cook in batches for 4 minutes per side, or until browned, adding more oil to the pan if necessary. Remove from the heat and set aside.

5. In a small bowl, mix together the ¼ cup (60 ml) soy sauce, brown sugar, 1 teaspoon garlic, ¼ teaspoon sesame oil, gochujang, 1 teaspoon lemon juice, ½ teaspoon agave, and water until well combined.

6. Add the sauce to a large saucepan over medium-low heat. Once the sauce starts to bubble, add the cooked tofu and stir, making sure to cover and submerge the tofu in the sauce. Cook for 3 minutes. Remove the braised tofu from the heat and set aside.

7. To make the sesame garlic bok choy: Bring a medium pot of water to a boil. Submerge the baby bok choy whole for 3 minutes. Remove with tongs and shake off the water.

8. In a separate large saucepan or skillet, combine the 1 teaspoon garlic, 2 teaspoons soy sauce, 1 teaspoon agave, 1 teaspoon lemon juice, ½ teaspoon olive oil, and ¼ teaspoon sesame oil. Mix together and heat over medium heat. Once warmed, add the bok choy and cook and stir until the bok choy is coated in the sauce.

9. Divide the tofu pieces among the plates, cover each piece with a spoonful of braised tofu sauce, and then add the sautéed mushrooms and scallions on top of each piece. Put the wasabi slaw next to the tofu and add a dollop of the spicy mayo in front of each piece. Lay a piece of bok choy (leaf and stalk) opposite the slaw on the plate.

 LOADED CHILI DOG

One bite of this fully loaded hot dog and you'll be taken back to getting nauseous on your favorite carnival ride, becoming frustrated playing the ring toss game that is obviously rigged, enjoying every second of the bright neon lights and screams of joy in the background, fighting off those killer klowns . . .

Yield: **1 serving** Prep time: **5 minutes** Cook time: **5 minutes**

DEADLY INGREDIENTS

1 vegan hot dog

1 tablespoon olive oil

1 large vegan hot dog bun
(or submarine-style roll)

¼ cup Chili Necronomicon Carne (page 69)

¼ cup Totally '80s Cheese Sauce (page 129)

¼ cup corn chips (such as Fritos)

2 tablespoons chopped scallions

1. In a small skillet, panfry the hotdog in the olive oil over medium-low heat for about 3 minutes, or until the outsides are crispy.

2. Toast both sides of the bun.

3. Put the hotdog in the bun and top it in this order: chili, cheese sauce, corn chips, and scallions.

SRIRACHA MAPLE FUNNEL CAKE BURGER

INSPIRED BY Carnival Horror

Amusement parks, carnivals, circuses, freak shows—there are plenty of horror shows and movies that incorporate these themes, including *It*, *The Lost Boys*, *American Horror Story: Freak Show*, *Killer Klowns from Outer Space*, *Child's Play 3*, and *Us*. This recipe was inspired by a favorite fair food: the funnel cake. It's fried, greasy, salty, and sweet, and worth the stomachache that may creep up on you.

Yield: **1 sandwich** Prep time: **15 minutes** Cook time: **30 minutes**

DEADLY INGREDIENTS

FUNNEL CAKES

1½ cups (180 g) all-purpose flour

1½ tablespoons baking powder

⅔ cup (135 g) sugar

½ cup (12 g) finely chopped fresh sage

¼ cup (7 g) finely chopped fresh rosemary

½ teaspoon sea salt

1½ cups (360 ml) unsweetened almond milk

1½ tablespoons lemon juice

2 teaspoons vanilla extract

4 cups (950 ml) oil, for frying

SRIRACHA MAPLE AIOLI

2 tablespoons vegan mayonnaise

½ teaspoon sriracha sauce

2 teaspoons pure maple syrup

½ teaspoons soy sauce

SANDWICH

1 vegan burger patty

2 slices vegan cheese of choice

2 strips Campfire Mushroom Bacon (page 132)

1. **To make the funnel cakes:** In a medium bowl, combine the flour, baking powder, sugar, sage, rosemary, and sea salt. Mix well.

2. In a large bowl, stir together the almond milk, lemon juice, and vanilla extract.

3. Add the dry ingredients to the wet ingredients and mix well until smooth. Allow the batter to rest for 10 to 15 minutes to give the milk time to soften the flour and dissolve any lumps.

4. Heat the oil in a large heavy-bottomed pot over high heat for 3 to 5 minutes before adding the batter. Line a plate with a paper towel and set aside.

(continued on page 56)

(continued from page 54)

5. Place the batter in a squeeze bottle. Squirt the batter in the oil in a circular motion over and over to create a thick, solid cake. Once you have a decent cake with a solid middle that is large enough to hold the burger patty, cook it for 2 to 3 minutes, until golden brown all over and you can flip it over. Cook it for another 2 to 3 minutes, then transfer to the prepared plate to drain and cool. Repeat this step for the second funnel cake (and additional funnel cakes if you have extra batter).

6. To make the sriracha maple aioli: In a small bowl, whisk together the mayonnaise, sriracha, maple syrup, and soy sauce until well blended. Refrigerate the sriracha-maple aioli in an airtight container for up to 2 weeks.

7. Cook the burger patty according to the package instructions.

8. To assemble, place the burger patty on a funnel cake and top with the cheese slices. Add the mushroom bacon strips, squirt the sriracha maple aioli over it, and top with the other funnel cake.

CHILDREN OF THE HOMINY

INSPIRED BY Children of the Corn

An ancient recipe from Gatlin, Nebraska, this pozole is a hearty soup that will even please He Who Walks Behind the Rows.

Yield: 6 servings Prep time: 20 minutes Cook time: 2 hours 15 minutes

DEADLY INGREDIENTS

SOUP
3 (14-ounce, or 397-g) cans jackfruit, drained and rinsed

Kosher salt, to taste

2 teaspoons freshly ground black pepper

2 cups (140 g) roughly chopped shitake mushrooms

1 large yellow onion, quartered

4 cloves garlic, sliced

1 teaspoon whole cloves

1 teaspoon cumin seeds

2 bay leaves

5 cups (1.2 L) vegetable broth

5 quarts (4.7 L) water

2 dried guajillo chiles, stem and seeds removed

3 dried chiles de arbol, stem and seeds removed

2 dried ancho chiles, stem and seeds removed

2 cups (475 ml) boiling water

3 (15-ounce, or 425-g) cans hominy, drained and rinsed

GARNISH
12 thin slices radish

⅓ avocado, thinly sliced and salted

Thinly shaved red onion, to taste

Fresh cilantro leaves, to taste

1. To make the soup: Season the jackfruit with the salt and pepper. In a large pot, combine the jackfruit, mushrooms, onion, garlic, cloves, cumin seeds, bay leaves, and broth over medium heat. Add the 5 quarts (4.7 L) water and bring the mixture to a boil, then cover and reduce the heat to a simmer. Let the soup simmer for 1 hour.

2. Meanwhile, place the dried chilies in a medium bowl and pour the boiling water over them. Let them soak for approximately 30 minutes.

3. Place the chiles and ¼ cup (60 ml) of their soaking liquid into a blender. Blend until smooth, adding more liquid if necessary.

4. Add the chile puree and the hominy to the pot with the jackfruit. Continue to simmer for another hour, then strain out the whole cloves and bay leaves and discard.

5. To serve, ladle the soup into bowls and fan the radish, avocado, and red onion on top. Dot with the cilantro leaves.

ALL HALLOWS' EVE LASAGNA

INSPIRED BY Trick 'r Treat

No need to worry about displeasing Sam because you won't be breaking any Halloween "rules" by making this pumpkin spinach lasagna.

Yield: 8 servings Prep time: 30 minutes Cook time: 1 hour

DEADLY INGREDIENTS

PUMPKIN BÉCHAMEL

2 teaspoons vegetable oil

½ cup (60 g) all-purpose flour

4 cups (950 ml) nondairy milk of choice

2 (15-ounce, or 425-g) cans pure pumpkin puree

2 teaspoons ground nutmeg

Salt and freshly ground black pepper, to taste

CASHEW AND SPINACH RICOTTA

1 cup (120 g) raw cashews

1 cup (240 ml) water

2 teaspoons vegetable oil

1 medium onion, finely diced

8 cloves garlic, minced

2 teaspoons all-purpose flour

16 ounces (454 g) spinach, cooked and chopped (can be frozen or canned; if frozen, thaw and drain before use)

1 teaspoon ground nutmeg

Salt and freshly ground black pepper, to taste

BREAD CRUMB TOPPING

1 cup (120 g) Italian-style bread crumbs

2 teaspoons olive oil

ASSEMBLY AND SERVING

15 no-boil lasagna noodles

2 teaspoons chopped fresh parsley or basil

1. To make the pumpkin béchamel: Heat the 2 teaspoons vegetable oil in a large saucepan over medium heat. Add the flour and whisk for 3 to 4 minutes, until the flour becomes fragrant.

2. Add the milk, whisking constantly to prevent lumps. Add the pumpkin and continue whisking until the mixture becomes smooth. Cook on medium heat for about 10 minutes, or until the sauce is thickened.

3. Add the 2 teaspoons nutmeg and salt and pepper. Stir until incorporated, then set aside to cool.

(continued on page 60)

(continued from page 59)

4. To make the cashew and spinach ricotta: In a blender, blend the cashews with the water until smooth.

5. Heat the 2 teaspoons vegetable oil in a large skillet over medium heat. Add the onion and garlic and cook until the onion is translucent.

6. Add the 2 teaspoons flour and continue to cook and stir for 3 to 4 minutes, until soft. Add the cashew cream and stir together. Add the chopped spinach and continue to cook for 3 minutes. Add the 1 teaspoon nutmeg, and season with salt and pepper. (If the cashew cream is too thick or sticks to the pan, add water, ¼ cup, or 60 ml, at a time until it reaches desired consistency.)

7. To make the bread crumb topping: In a small bowl, stir together the bread crumbs and olive oil.

8. Preheat the oven to 375°F (190°C; gas mark 5).

9. To assemble, spread a few ladles of the béchamel across the bottom of a 9 × 13-inch (23 × 33 cm) baking dish. Layer 5 of the lasagna noodles on top of the sauce. Spread about half of the ricotta across the noodles and cover it with about a third of the remaining béchamel. Layer 5 more noodles across the top. Spread the remaining ricotta across the top of the layer of noodles. Ladle half of the remaining béchamel over the ricotta. Layer the remaining 5 noodles across the top and cover with the remaining béchamel. Top evenly with the bread crumb topping.

10. Cover with aluminum foil and bake for 30 minutes. Remove the foil and bake for an additional 30 minutes, or until the bread crumbs are golden brown. Let stand for 10 minutes before slicing and serving.

PUMPKINHEAD SOUP

INSPIRED BY Pumpkinhead

Let's give them "pumpkin" to talk about! This soup, made in an Instant Pot, will satisfy those pumpkin cravings on chilly autumn nights.

Yield: 2 to 4 servings **Prep time:** 15 minutes **Cook time:** 40 minutes

DEADLY INGREDIENTS

4 tablespoons olive oil, divided

1 medium red onion, finely chopped

3 cups (700 ml) vegetable broth

2 (15-ounce, or 425-g) cans pure pumpkin puree

1 (13.5-ounce, or 400 ml) can coconut milk

15 ounces (445 ml) unsweetened cashew milk

¼ cup (55 g) packed brown sugar

1 teaspoon ground cinnamon

¼ teaspoon white pepper

½ teaspoon ground ginger

¼ teaspoon cayenne pepper

¼ teaspoon Chinese five-spice powder

3 tablespoons Bragg Liquid Aminos

Slices bread of choice, for serving (optional)

1. In a large skillet, heat 2 tablespoons of the olive oil over medium heat. Add the onion and cook until browned.

2. Put the cooked onion, broth, pumpkin puree, coconut milk, cashew milk, brown sugar, cinnamon, pepper, ginger, cayenne, five-spice powder, liquid aminos, and remaining 2 tablespoons olive oil, into an Instant Pot. Whisk together well. Cook on the Soup/Broth setting, or for 20 to 30 minutes on high pressure and high heat, releasing the pressure manually.

3. Ladle the soup into bowls while hot and serve with bread slices (if using).

DINNER IN THE DARK

INSPIRED BY **Alone in the Dark**

When the power goes out, let's hope all you have to worry about is eating this warming meal and not any dangerous criminals on the loose.

Yield: **2 to 4 servings** Prep time: **20 minutes** Cook time: **1 hour 15 minutes**

DEADLY INGREDIENTS

ROASTED VEGETABLES

1 cup (150 g) chopped red potatoes

1 cup (115 g) chopped red onion

2 cups (480 g) rainbow baby carrots

1 (8-ounce, or 227-g) package whole portobello mushrooms

1 cup (140 g) chopped butternut squash

¼ cup (60 ml) olive oil

1½ teaspoons salt

½ teaspoon ground cinnamon

1 tablespoon finely chopped garlic

1 teaspoon agave syrup

¼ cup (7 g) finely chopped fresh rosemary

¼ cup (6 g) finely chopped fresh sage

¼ cup (25 g) chopped scallions

¼ teaspoon cayenne pepper

¼ cup (60 ml) water

GARLIC WHIPPED MASHED POTATOES

6 whole red potatoes

Salt, for the cooking water

¼ cup (60 ml) unsweetened nut milk of choice

1 teaspoon agave syrup

1 teaspoon finely chopped garlic

1 teaspoon salt

SERVING

¼ cup (60 ml) Truffle Glaze (page 128)

I. To make the roasted vegetables: Preheat the oven to 400°F (205°C; gas mark 6).

2. In a large bowl, combine the 1 cup (150 g) chopped potatoes, onion, carrots, mushrooms, and squash. Add the olive oil, 1½ teaspoons salt, cinnamon, 1 tablespoon garlic, agave, rosemary, sage, scallions, and cayenne. Toss to coat the vegetables evenly, then transfer to a baking sheet.

3. Add the water to the base of the pan and roast uncovered for 15 minutes. Reduce the oven temperature to 375°F (190°C; gas mark 5) and roast for another 30 minutes, or until the vegetables are tender enough to pierce with a fork. (If the edges of the vegetables start to burn, cover the pan with foil.)

4. Meanwhile, make the garlic whipped mashed potatoes: In a large pot, bring enough salted water to a boil to submerge the whole unpeeled potatoes. Once boiling, add the potatoes and boil for about 20 minutes, or until soft and ready to mash.

5. Drain the potatoes and transfer them to a large bowl. Mash them with their skins. Add the milk, agave, 1 teaspoon garlic, and 1 teaspoon salt, then use a hand mixer to whip the potatoes until creamy.

6. Put a large dollop of the potatoes onto each plate and place some of the roasted vegetable medley on top. Finish by drizzling the truffle glaze over the top of the veggies.

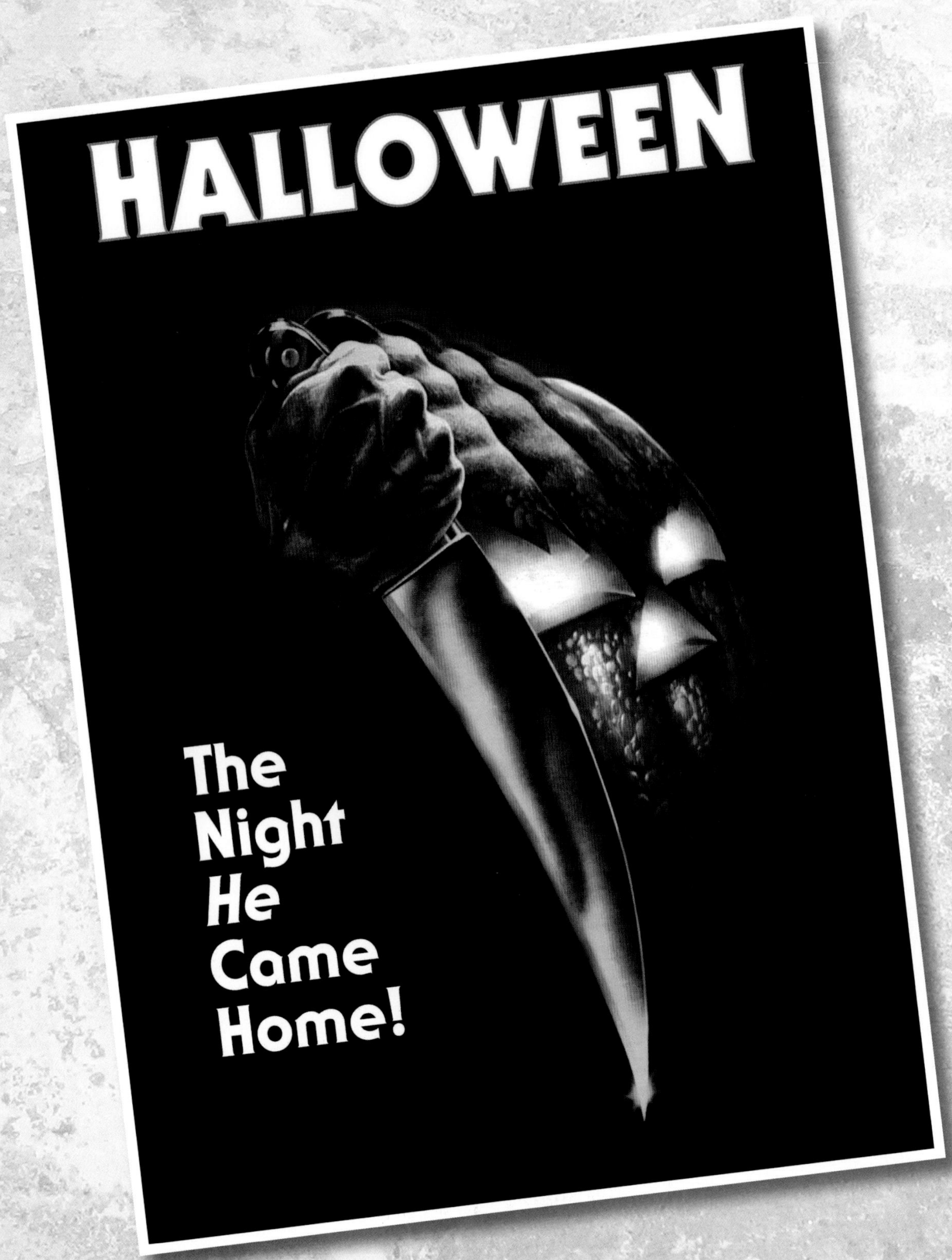
HALLOWEEN
The Night He Came Home!

HADDONFRIED STEAK

INSPIRED BY Halloween

There's nothing like returning home for a home-cooked meal . . . or murder if you're Michael Myers.

Yield: 2 to 4 servings **Prep time:** 30 minutes **Cook time:** 1 hour

DEADLY INGREDIENTS

CHICKEN CUTLETS
1 (8-ounce, or 227-g) package tempeh

Oil, for frying

BREADING
¾ cup (180 ml) unsweetened almond milk

2¼ teaspoons apple cider vinegar

1 cup (120 g) all-purpose flour

1 cup (120 g) cornstarch

1 teaspoon salt

1 teaspoon dried basil

1½ teaspoons Old Bay Seasoning

1 teaspoon dried oregano

1½ teaspoons celery salt

1½ teaspoons freshly ground black pepper

1½ teaspoons ground yellow mustard

4 tablespoons smoked paprika

1 tablespoon garlic salt

1½ teaspoons ground ginger

1 tablespoon white pepper

1½ tablespoons Ajinomoto (or MSG)

CHEESY MASHED POTATOES
6 quarts (5.7 L) water

4 large Idaho potatoes, peeled

Salt, for cooking water

2 tablespoons celery salt

1 cup (240 g) vegan sour cream

1 cup (120 g) shredded vegan
  cheddar cheese

2 teaspoons white pepper

1 tablespoon garlic powder

1 teaspoon onion powder

1 scallion, finely chopped

CARAMELIZED ONION RAGÙ
1 red bell pepper

½ cup (120 ml) plus 1 tablespoon oil, divided

Salt, to taste

1 red onion, diced

3 cups (180 g) chopped
  cremini mushrooms

Onion salt, to taste

Freshly ground black pepper, to taste

GRAVY
2 cups (475 ml) vegetable broth

¼ cup (15 g) nutritional yeast

1 teaspoon Dijon mustard

¼ cup (30 g) all-purpose flour

1 teaspoon onion powder

½ teaspoon garlic powder

1 tablespoon tamari

(continued on page 66)

(continued from page 65)

I. To make the chicken cutlets: Cut the tempeh into large slices, around ½ inch (1 cm) thick.

2. To make the breading: In a medium bowl, stir together the almond milk and apple cider vinegar to create a vegan buttermilk.

3. In a large bowl, mix together the 2 cups (240 g) flour, cornstarch, salt, dried basil, Old Bay Seasoning, dried oregano, 1 tablespoon celery salt, black pepper, ground mustard, paprika, garlic salt, ground ginger, 2 teaspoons white pepper, and Ajinomoto until thoroughly combined. Divide the dry mixture equally between two medium bowls.

4. Heat 2 inches (5 cm) of oil in a large heavy-bottomed pot to 350°F (175°C). Line a plate with a paper towel and set aside.

5. Place the tempeh into one of the dry-mixture bowls, then into the buttermilk, and then into the other dry-mixture bowl. Working in batches, deep-fry the tempeh for 3 minutes, until browned, then transfer to the prepared plate to drain.

6. To make the mashed potatoes: Add the water and salt to a large pot and bring to a boil. Cut the potatoes into similarly sized pieces so that they cook evenly. Rinse the pieces before cooking.

7. Once boiling, add the potatoes to the pot and boil for 15 to 20 minutes, until tender enough to pierce with a fork. Drain them in a colander and let them cool for or 8 minutes.

8. Transfer the potatoes to a large bowl and combine with the 2 tablespoons celery salt, sour cream, shredded cheddar, 2 teaspoons white pepper, 1 tablespoon garlic powder, 1 teaspoon onion powder, and scallion. Mash the potatoes. Season to taste.

9. To make the caramelized onion ragù: Rub the bell pepper with 1 tablespoon of the oil and season with salt. Roast it on an open flame from a stovetop burner (or use a grill). Once all sides are blackened, transfer the pepper to a bowl and cover it with plastic wrap to cool and steam for 10 minutes. Remove the skin and seeds, then dice the pepper.

10. In a large skillet, heat ¼ cup (60 ml) of the oil over medium to high heat. Add the onion and cook, stirring every 2 minutes with a wooden spoon. In a separate large skillet, heat the remaining ¼ cup (60 ml) oil over medium to high heat. Add the mushrooms and cook, stirring every 2 minutes with a wooden spoon. After about

15 to 20 minutes, you should have nice caramelization on both the onions and the mushrooms. Mix together the onions, mushrooms, and roasted pepper and season with onion salt and black pepper.

11. To make the gravy: In a medium saucepan, combine the vegetable broth, nutritional yeast, Dijon, ¼ cup (30 g) flour, 1 teaspoon onion powder, ½ teaspoon garlic powder, and tamari over medium heat. Whisk until the mixture thickens to a gravy consistency. Remove from the heat.

12. Scoop some of the cheesy mashed potatoes onto each plate, top with a chicken cutlet, and smother everything with gravy and caramelized onion ragù.

CHILI NECRONOMICON CARNE

INSPIRED BY The Evil Dead

Meaty, spicy, and hearty, and I'm not just talking about Ash Williams. This chili, made in an Instant Pot, pairs great with Evil Bread and Totally '80s Cheese Sauce.

Yield: 4 servings Prep time: 15 minutes Cook time: 20 minutes

DEADLY INGREDIENTS

2 (14.5-ounce, or 411-g) cans stewed tomatoes

1 (14.5-ounce, or 411-g) can diced zesty chili-style tomatoes (such as Del Monte)

1 (10-ounce, or 283-g) can mild diced tomatoes and green chilies (such as Ro-Tel Original)

1 large bell pepper, roughly chopped

1 medium red onion, diced

2 teaspoons chili powder

1 teaspoon ground cumin

½ teaspoon ground mustard

2 teaspoons Cajun seasoning

1 teaspoon white pepper

½ teaspoon cayenne pepper

3 tablespoons agave syrup

1½ teaspoons sea salt

1 (15-ounce, or 425-g) can black beans

1 (15-ounce, or 425-g) can kidney beans

1 (15.25-ounce, or 432-g) can whole kernel corn, drained

Evil Bread (page 32), for serving

Finely chopped onion, for serving (optional)

Vegan sour cream, for serving (optional)

Totally '80s Cheese Sauce (page 129), for serving

1. Put the diced tomatoes, bell pepper, onion, chili powder, cumin, ground mustard, Cajun seasoning, white pepper, cayenne, agave, and salt into an Instant Pot. Use a potato masher to break up the tomatoes. Then add the beans and corn. Stir everything together. Cook on the Bean/Chili setting, or about 20 minutes on high pressure, releasing the pressure manually.

2. Ladle the chili into bowls, drizzle with the cheese sauce, and top with a piece of Evil Bread. Serve with chopped onion (if using), sour cream (if using), and totally '80s cheese sauce (if using) for topping options.

HELL BURGER

INSPIRED BY Hellraiser

Welcome to hell. Your mouth will thank you! This burger combines plenty of heat and all the fixings. Once you open the box to this plate there's no turning back . . .

Yield: 1 sandwich Prep time: 15 minutes Cook time: 1 hour 30 minutes

DEADLY INGREDIENTS

2 vegan burger patties

1 teaspoon Vamp Paste (page 128)

1 large vegan burger bun

1 tablespoon Tex-Mex Ranch (page 124)

1½ teaspoons Hell Sauce (page 126)

2 slices vegan pepper jack cheese

12 slices Cowboy Candy (page 133)

4 strips Campfire Mushroom Bacon (page 132)

2 tablespoons Totally '80's Cheese Sauce (page 129)

1 tablespoon Sweet Onion Jam (page 130)

1. Start by making sure you have the all the sauces and staples for this burger made in advance.

2. Cook the burger patties according to the package instructions, then remove from the heat and set aside.

3. Spread the vamp paste on the insides of both halves of the hamburger bun. Heat a small skillet over medium heat and toast the bun, cut sides down, until the insides are golden brown, about 2 to 3 minutes. Transfer the bun to a plate.

4. To assemble, spread some Tex-Mex ranch on the bottom bun, then place a patty on top. Spread 1½ teaspoons of the hell sauce on top of the patty. Place a slice of pepper jack on the patty followed by 6 slices of the cowboy candy, 2 strips of the mushroom bacon, then 1 tablespoon of the cheese sauce. Place the remaining patty on top and repeat the process, finishing with the sweet onion jam. Spread the rest of the ranch on the inside of the top bun, then gently place the bun on top of the burger.

SET THE SCENE

When ready to serve, push 8 to 10 stainless steel skewers (at least 8 inches, or 20 cm, long) into the top bun all the way through the burger to hold everything in place and to look like Pinhead. Place 2 to 4 pieces of small stainless-steel chain around the burger on the plate to complete the scene. Watch your favorite Hellraiser movie and enjoy!

PASTAGEIST

INSPIRED BY Poltergeist

You won't "go into the light" with this dish made with black bean pasta and homemade Bolognese sauce beckoning you to the dinner table.

Yield: **2 servings** Prep time: **20 minutes** Cook time: **4 hours 30 minutes**

DEADLY INGREDIENTS

BOLOGNESE

1 package vegan ground beef

1 tablespoon Italian seasoning

3 cups (750 g) Blood and Basil Sauce
(page 131) or marinara sauce of choice

VEGETABLES

3 tablespoons oil, divided

1 zucchini

Salt and freshly ground black pepper, to taste

2 cups (120 g) chopped cremini mushrooms

PASTA

8 ounces (227 g) black bean spaghetti

GARNISH

1 teaspoon olive oil

10 baby heirloom tomatoes

Salt and freshly ground black pepper, to taste

2 tablespoons finely chopped fresh basil

1 lemon for zesting

Vegan Parmesan cheese, to taste

1 tablespoon crispy fried shallots (optional)

1 tablespoon capers, drained (optional)

1. To make the Bolognese: Season the ground beef with the Italian seasoning. In a medium saucepan, cook the meat according to the package instructions, then add the blood and basil sauce to the pan and let it reduce while stirring for 20 minutes.

2. To make the vegetables: Slice the zucchini into thin, noodle-type cuts to match the shape of the spaghetti. In a large skillet, heat 1½ tablespoons of the oil over low to medium heat. Add the zucchini and cook for 3 to 5 minutes, stirring occasionally, until tender enough to pierce with a fork. Season with salt and pepper. Transfer to a paper towel–lined plate to soak up the excess juice.

3. Heat the remaining 1½ tablespoons oil in the same pan over low to medium heat. Add the mushrooms and cook for 5 to 7 minutes, until tender. Season with salt and pepper. Transfer to a paper towel–lined plate to soak up the excess juice.

4. To make the pasta: Cook the pasta according to the package instructions, then drain and rinse with cold water.

5. To make the garnish: In a separate large skillet, heat the 1 teaspoon olive oil over medium to high heat. Add the tomatoes and cook for 1 minute, or until blistered and soft. Season with salt and pepper.

6. Toss the pasta with the zucchini and mushrooms, then place in a bowl. Top the pasta with the Bolognese sauce and garnish with the blistered tomatoes, fresh basil, lemon zest, Parmesan, crispy shallots (if using), and capers (if using).

NOTE
Crispy fried shallots can be purchased online and at Asian markets. There are also plenty of recipes online to make your own.

⋙ SPAGHETTI ⋘ DOLCE PICCANTE

INSPIRED BY Deep Red

Take a deep dive into the world of Italian giallo films while enjoying this spicy-sweet pasta dish.

Yield: 2 to 4 servings   Prep time: 15 minutes   Cook time: 30 minutes

DEADLY INGREDIENTS

QUICK RED WINE MARINARA

⅓ cup (80 ml) Merlot

1 tablespoon lemon juice

1 (15-ounce, or 425-g) can Italian-style stewed tomatoes

1 (15-ounce, or 425-g) can whole peeled tomatoes

2 tablespoons soy sauce

1 teaspoon chopped garlic

2 tablespoons agave syrup

¼ cup (6 g) chopped fresh sage

¼ cup (7 g) chopped fresh rosemary

PASTA

8 ounces (227 g) cups spaghetti

TOMATO, ROASTED RED PEPPER, AND ONION BRUSCHETTA

½ cup (75 g) chopped cherry tomatoes

¼ cup (25 g) chopped scallions

¼ cup (35 g) chopped roasted red peppers

1 tablespoon olive oil

1 teaspoon balsamic vinegar

1 teaspoon agave syrup

½ teaspoon sea salt

1 tablespoon lemon juice

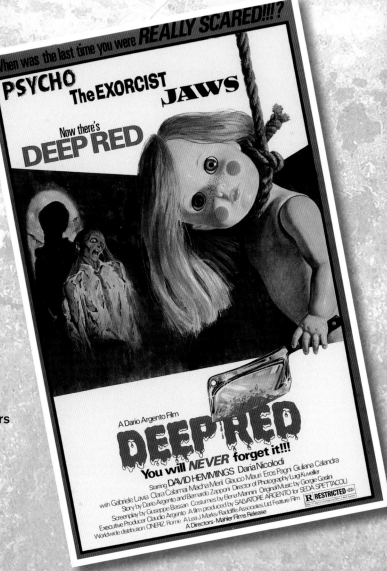

1. To make the quick red wine marinara: In a food processor, combine the red wine, lemon juice, stewed tomatoes, peeled tomatoes, soy sauce, garlic, 2 tablespoons agave, sage, and rosemary. Process for 2 minutes.

2. Transfer the mixture to a medium saucepan and heat over medium heat for 15 to 20 minutes at a slow boil, stirring frequently.

3. To make the pasta: Cook the spaghetti according to the package instructions, drain, and rinse with cold water.

4. To make the tomato, roasted red pepper, and onion bruschetta: In a medium bowl, combine the cherry tomatoes, scallions, red peppers, olive oil, balsamic vinegar, 1 teaspoon agave, sea salt, and lemon juice.

5. In a large bowl toss the cooked pasta with the red wine sauce.

6. Serve the pasta in bowls and top with the bruschetta.

SLAY-WORTHY MUSHROOM CARBONARA

INSPIRED BY The New York Ripper

Start spreading the news that this pasta dish is worth ripping into.

Yield: 2 to 4 servings   **Prep time:** 20 minutes   **Cook time:** 30 minutes

DEADLY INGREDIENTS

PASTA
8 ounces (227 g) cups pasta (such as rotini ziti, penne, or rigatoni)

2 tablespoons olive oil

MUSHROOMS
8 ounces (227 g) portobello mushrooms, sliced

½ cup (58 g) chopped red onion

2 tablespoons Bragg Liquid Aminos

1½ tablespoons liquid smoke

¼ cup (60 ml) water

2 tablespoons olive oil

SAUCE
2 (13.5-ounce, or 400-ml) cans unsweetened coconut milk

1 avocado, pitted and peeled

1 tablespoon finely chopped fresh sage

1 tablespoon finely chopped fresh rosemary

1 tablespoon finely chopped garlic

1 teaspoon salt

2 tablespoons lemon juice

1 (5.29-ounce, or 150-g) block Violife Just Like Parmesan cheese, roughly chopped

1 to 3 tablespoons Wondra Quick-Mixing Flour, to thicken (if needed)

SERVING
Truffle Glaze (page 128), to taste

1. To make the pasta: Cook the pasta according to package instructions just beyond al dente, drain, and rinse with cool water. Return the pasta to the pot and stir in 2 tablespoons olive oil to coat the pasta so that it doesn't stick together. Set aside.

2. To make the mushrooms: In a medium pan, combine the mushrooms, onion, liquid aminos, liquid smoke, water, and 2 tablespoons olive oil over medium-low heat. Cook for 5 to 7 minutes, stirring frequently, until the mushrooms and onions start to brown and reduce. Remove from the heat and set aside.

3. To make the sauce: In a food processor, combine the coconut milk, avocado, sage, rosemary, garlic, salt, lemon juice, and chopped Parmesan. Process until smooth and creamy, about 90 seconds.

4. Transfer the sauce to a medium saucepan and heat over medium-low heat, stirring frequently, until bubbling. Continue stirring frequently, allowing the sauce to bubble for 3 to 5 minutes to release the flavors. If the sauce needs thickening, slowly add the Wondra Flour. Remove from the heat and set aside.

5. Mix the pasta with a liberal amount of the sauce, making sure to toss it to coat the pasta thoroughly.

6. Put the pasta into bowls, spoon some of the mushrooms on top, and drizzle with the truffle glaze.

"All work and no play make Jack a dull boy."
The Shining, 1980.

DEPRAVED DESSERTS

☠IT FLOATS☠

INSPICED BY *Stephen King's It*

You'll be floating too after downing this irresistible beverage that combines root beer and spiced rum–soaked black cherries with your favorite vegan vanilla ice cream. It would be "wise" of you to savor every sip.

Yield: **1 serving** Prep time: **40 minutes** (plus 2 hours soaking time)

DEADLY INGREDIENTS

SPICED RUM–SOAKED BLACK CHERRIES
1 cup (140 g) pitted black cherries

1 cup (240 ml) spiced rum

¼ cup (50 g) granulated sugar

CHERRY BLOOD SYRUP
1 cup (240 ml) cherry juice

1 cup (125 g) confectioners' sugar

½ teaspoon cayenne pepper

ROOT BEER FLOAT
¾ cup (180 ml) craft bottled root beer

1 or 2 scoops vegan vanilla ice cream

Vegan whipped topping, for serving

1. **To make the spiced rum–soaked black cherries:** In a large saucepan, heat the black cherries, spiced rum, and granulated sugar over medium heat until warmed but not boiling. Remove from the heat and let soak in the pan for 2 hours. Do not drain. Refrigerate in an airtight container for up to 2 weeks.

2. **To make the cherry blood syrup:** In a medium saucepan, bring the cherry juice, confectioners' sugar, and cayenne to a boil over medium heat, stirring frequently until a syrup forms. Let the mixture cool, then transfer it to a squeeze bottle or another container for drizzling.

3. **To make the root beer float:** Frost your favorite large mug or glass (12 to 16 ounces, or 350 to 475 ml) in the freezer for 30 minutes.

4. Pour the root beer into the frosted mug, then add the ice cream in scoops.

5. Top with 3 or 4 of the spiced rum–soaked black cherries and whipped topping.

6. Drizzle with the cherry blood syrup.

☠ PEANUT BUTTER POPCORN ☠

INSPIRED BY Scream

"Do you like scary movies?" Then make watching them even more enjoyable with this peanut-buttery twist on a favorite movie snack—it's salty, sweet, and just as nutty as Ghostface.

Yield: 2 **servings** Prep time: 5 minutes Cook time: 15 minutes

DEADLY INGREDIENTS

1 (3.2-ounce, or 90-g) bag microwave popcorn, no butter (vegan)

¼ cup (65 g) smooth peanut butter

2 tablespoons Vegan Butter (page 127) or vegan butter of choice

2 tablespoons agave syrup

½ teaspoon salt

1. Make the popcorn following the package instructions. Set aside.

2. In a large saucepan, combine the peanut butter, butter, agave syrup, and salt over medium heat, stirring frequently until melted.

3. Pour the prepared popcorn into the peanut butter mixture, remove the pan from the heat, and stir well, tossing until all the popcorn is well coated.

4. Pour the popcorn into a large bowl and serve immediately.

SET THE SCENE

In a large popcorn container, place a piece of Styrofoam (to hold a dull knife or prop knife). Press the knife into the foam with the handle up and the blade down. Be sure to use a large knife but not a sharp one, as you could cut your hand serving. Once the knife is affixed to the foam, pour the popcorn over the top so that it fills up and hides the Styrofoam. If this is too complicated, just dump the popcorn into a bowl, watch Scream, and enjoy!

☠KILLER CHERRY☠ CRUMB PIE

INSPIRED BY Slasher Films

Be "cherry" afraid! There's nothing more satisfying than pairing this classic dessert with a good slasher film.

Yield: 8 servings **Prep time:** 15 minutes **Cook time:** 2 hours

DEADLY INGREDIENTS

FILLING
6 cups (840 g) pitted fresh or frozen sweet dark cherries (never canned!)

1 cup (240 ml) water

⅓ cup (112 g) agave syrup

1 teaspoon salt

VEGAN PIECRUST
1½ cups (180 g) all-purpose flour, plus more for the work surface

2 teaspoons brown sugar

½ teaspoon salt

¼ cup (56 g) cold Vegan Butter (page 127) or vegan butter of choice, cubed

¼ cup (48 g) cold vegetable shortening

3 tablespoons ice water, plus more if needed

VEGAN PIE CRUMBS
½ cup (112 g) Vegan Butter (page 127) or vegan butter of choice, melted

½ cup (100 g) granulated sugar

1 cup (120 g) all-purpose flour

1. To make the filling: In a large saucepan, combine the cherries, water, agave, and 1 teaspoon salt. Cook over medium heat for 6 to 10 minutes, until the mixture has bubbled for at least 2 minutes and a thick syrup (like a thick pancake syrup) has formed. Remove from the heat and allow to cool completely, about 30 minutes.

2. To make the crust: Combine the 1½ cups (180 g) flour, brown sugar, and ½ teaspoon salt in a food processor and process for a few seconds. Add the ¼ cup (56 g) cold butter and shortening and process for a few seconds.

3. Add the ice water. Process again, and when it begins to clump together, stop. Add a little more water if needed, a teaspoon at a time.

4. Transfer the dough to a lightly floured surface and shape it into a ball.

5. Using a rolling pin, roll the dough into a 10- to 12-inch (25 to 30 cm) circle, then gently transfer it to an 8-inch (20 cm) round pie plate. Press into the pie plate and crimp the edges. Set aside. (If not planning to use the crust immediately, cover the dough in the pie plate and refrigerate for up to 3 days.)

6. Preheat the oven to 350°F (175°C; gas mark 4).

7. To make the crumbs: In a large bowl, combine the melted butter with the granulated sugar and 1 cup (120 g) flour. Stir and smash the mixture with a fork until the ingredients start to form granules and clumps.

8. Pour the cooled filling into the piecrust, top with the crumbs (the whole top should be covered about ½ inch (1 cm) thick.

9. Bake for 30 to 40 minutes, until the edges of the crust are golden brown and the crumbs on top are light to medium brown (some ovens may cook faster). Remove from the oven and allow to cool before slicing.

NOTE

To make a double-crust pie, double the ingredient amounts for the vegan piecrust.

☠BLOOD-SOAKED LOAF☠

INSPIRED BY Andy Warhol's Blood for Dracula

This isn't your standard cake—it's drenched in red wine blood and filled with blood orange zest—so passing up on this delectable treat would be a grave mi-stake.

Yield: 8 servings Prep time: 15 minutes Cook time: 1 hour 30 minutes

DEADLY INGREDIENTS

RED WINE BLOOD

½ cup (120 ml) Chianti, divided, plus more as needed

¼ cup (50 g) sugar

1 tablespoon peppercorns

ITALIAN (BLOOD) ORANGE OLIVE OIL CAKE

1½ cups (180 g) all-purpose flour

⅓ cup (65 g) sugar

1½ teaspoons baking powder

½ teaspoon baking soda

½ teaspoon salt

Zest of 1 blood orange (or a regular orange)

⅓ cup (80 ml) extra-virgin olive oil

½ cup (120 ml) unsweetened nondairy milk

⅓ cup (112 g) agave syrup

1 tablespoon apple cider vinegar

2 teaspoons vanilla extract

I. To make the red wine blood: In a small saucepan, combine the Chianti, ¼ cup (50 g) sugar, and the peppercorns over medium-high heat, stirring until the sugar dissolves.

2. Bring the mixture to a boil, and then reduce the heat to a simmer until the mixture has reduced to about a third, 15 to 20 minutes. It should be syrupy, but don't worry if it's too thick; you can thin it down with additional wine later.

3. Allow the red wine reduction to cool completely in the refrigerator but keep an eye on the consistency. Add more wine until the consistency is like maple syrup. Strain the peppercorns.

4. To make the Italian (blood) orange olive oil cake: Preheat the oven to 350°F (175°C; gas mark 4). Grease an 8½ × 4½-inch (22 × 11 cm) loaf pan. Cut a piece of parchment paper to fit the bottom and long sides of the pan with a little overhang.

5. In a medium bowl, whisk together the flour, ⅓ cup (65 g) sugar, baking powder, baking soda, salt, and orange zest.

6. In a separate small bowl, whisk together the olive oil, milk, agave, vinegar, and vanilla.

7. Add the wet ingredients to the dry ingredients and stir with a spatula until incorporated, about 1 minute. Spread the batter in the prepared pan.

8. Bake on the center rack for about 45 minutes, or until the cake is dark golden brown and a toothpick inserted into the center comes out clean.

9. Let the cake cool in the pan on a cooling rack for 10 minutes, and then, using the parchment paper overhang, lift the cake out of the pan and let it cool on the rack to room temperature.

10. Place the loaf on a generous-size piece of new parchment paper, drizzle with about a quarter of the red wine blood (mainly for effect at this point), and loosely wrap the loaf like a package.

11. To serve, place the package on a dish or board, open it, cut it into slices, and plate them. Let the diners drizzle more red wine blood to taste.

☠ BLOOD (ORANGE) ☠ CHEESECAKE TRIFLE

INSPIRED BY Dexter

No gloves and plastic wrap are required to make this light and airy trifle that only has a little blood spatter.

Yield: 8 servings Prep time: 20 minutes Cook time: 1 hour 30 minutes

DEADLY INGREDIENTS

CAKE

3 cups (390 g) cake flour

1 tablespoon baking powder

½ teaspoon salt

½ large banana

1¼ cups (300 ml) unsweetened nondairy milk, divided

2 teaspoons apple cider vinegar

½ cup (115 g) Vegan Butter (page 127) or vegan butter of choice, softened

½ cup (120 ml) melted coconut oil

1½ cups (300 g) granulated sugar

1 tablespoon vanilla extract

CHEESECAKE FILLING

Approximately 16 ounces (454 g) vegan cream cheese

1½ cups (190 g) confectioners' sugar

3 tablespoons lemon juice

1 tablespoon vanilla extract

SERVING

1 blood orange, peeled and sliced

Vegan whipped topping

1. **To make the cake:** Preheat the oven to 350°F (175°C; gas mark 4). Grease a 9 × 13-inch (23 × 33 cm) cake pan and set aside.

2. Whisk together the flour, baking powder, and salt in a medium bowl.

3. In a small bowl, cream the banana and ¼ cup (60 ml) of the milk together until it resembles whipped egg whites (an immersion blender works well for this).

4. Combine the remaining 1 cup (240 ml) milk, vinegar, butter, coconut oil, granulated sugar, and vanilla extract in a large bowl. Mix well. Stir in the creamed banana.

5. Add the dry ingredients to the wet ingredients and, using a stand or hand mixer, mix for 2 minutes on medium speed, or until the batter is smooth. Pour the batter into the prepared pan.

(continued on page 90)

(continued from page 89)

6. Bake for 30 to 35 minutes, until a toothpick inserted into the center comes out clean. Let cool in the pan.

7. To make the cheesecake filling: Using a stand or hand mixer, mix all the cheesecake filling ingredients on high speed for about 2 minutes, or until it starts to get fluffy like whipped cream.

8. Transfer the mixture to a container with a lid and refrigerate.

9. To assemble, put a dollop of the cheesecake filling into the bottoms of tall glasses. On top of that, crumble or cube some of the cooled cake, repeating this layering of cheesecake and crumbled cake a couple of times. Add the blood orange slices either in the layers or on top. Chill for 30 minutes. Top with whipped cream to serve.

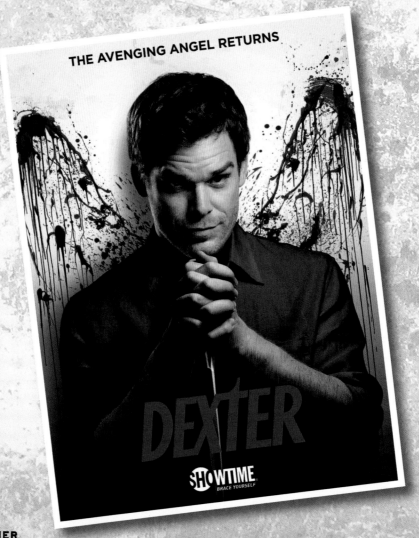

☠SWEET-AND-SOUR MAGGOTS☠

INSPIRED BY The Lost Boys

"They're only noodles," and these maggots are only marzipan, right?

Yield: 6 to 8 servings Prep time: **20 minutes** Cook time: **2 hours**

DEADLY INGREDIENTS

MARZIPAN
6 ounces (170 g) good quality store-bought marzipan, or make it from scratch:

1 cup (115 g) almond flour

1 cup (125 g) confectioners' sugar, plus more if needed

1 tablespoon water

1 teaspoon almond extract (optional)

Ground cinnamon, for dusting

ORANGE GELATIN
Use a 3-ounce (85 g) package store-bought vegan orange gelatin powder, or make it from scratch:

1 cup (240 ml) orange juice

1/4 cup (50 g) granulated sugar

1 teaspoon finely chopped orange zest

2 teaspoons agar-agar powder

1/4 cup (60 ml) water

GINGER CAKE
1/3 cup (80 ml) olive oil, plus more for greasing the pan

1 cup (120 g) all-purpose flour

1 cup (120 g) white whole wheat flour

3/4 teaspoon baking soda

1 1/2 teaspoons ground ginger

1 teaspoon ground cinnamon

1/4 teaspoon ground nutmeg

1/2 teaspoon fine sea salt

1/4 teaspoon black pepper

1 cup (244 g) unsweetened applesauce

1/3 cup (80 ml) unsulfured molasses

1/2 cup (168 g) agave syrup

1 1/2 teaspoons vanilla extract

DRIZZLE
1/2 cup (168 g) agave syrup

Zest of 1 orange

1. To make the marzipan: On a large cutting board, mound the almond flour and confectioners' sugar. Make a hollow in the center and add the 1 tablespoon water and almond extract (if using).

2. Using a dough scraper, push the dry ingredients in from the edges to the center and make cutting movements to mix.

3. Repeat until the consistency changes from dry to crumbly, then using your hands, knead the dough until the marzipan has a smooth consistency and is not sticky. (Add more confectioners' sugar if it's too sticky.)

(continued on page 92)

(continued from page 91)

4. To make the orange gelatin: In a medium bowl, stir together the orange juice, granulated sugar, and 1 teaspoon orange zest. Set aside.

5. Put the agar agar in a medium saucepan, add the ¼ cup water, and bring the mixture to a boil.

6. While the water is boiling, cook, stirring, until a clear liquid without any lumps forms, about 5 minutes. Add the orange juice mixture, stirring continuously. Pour a thin layer into a shallow dish or tray and let set at room temperature.

7. To make the ginger cake: Preheat the oven to 350°F (175°C; gas mark 4). Line an 8 × 8-inch (20 × 20 cm) baking dish with parchment paper with a little overhang. Grease lightly with olive oil and set aside.

8. In a large bowl, whisk together the flours, baking soda, ginger, cinnamon, nutmeg, sea salt, and pepper. 9. In a medium bowl, whisk together the applesauce, ⅓ cup (80 ml) olive oil, molasses, ½ cup (168 g) honey, and vanilla until well combined.

9. Add the wet ingredients to the dry ingredients and mix gently. Transfer the batter to the prepared pan and spread evenly.

10. Bake for about 30 minutes, or until a toothpick inserted into the middle of the cake comes out clean. Set the pan on a wire rack to cool completely, then remove the cake from the pan.

11. To make the drizzle: Warm the ½ cup (168 g) honey and orange zest in a pan, then remove it from the heat and let it steep for about 10 minutes. Strain out the zest and brush the cake with the warm, orange-flavored honey.

12. To make the maggots: Using a ricer or craft extruder, make marzipan "snakes," then cut the snakes into maggot-size lengths, bend them slightly, and smooth the ends. You can also shape pea-size balls of marzipan into maggots by hand-rolling each ball into a long football shape, long enough to bend it to a curve. This will take time but it's worth it.

13. Once you have made the desired number of maggots, let them dry for a couple of hours, then dust or toss them in cinnamon to add "shading." (If you want to add that

SET THE SCENE
Serve in Chinese takeout containers to impress any fan of this classic vampire film.

extra touch of realism, score vertical lines along the maggots' "bodies" before dusting them in cinnamon.) Start with a little cinnamon at a time and add more to taste or to darken the color. You want a lightly shaded effect, not too dark.

14. In bowls, crumble chunks of the ginger cake (to resemble chicken or pork), add a few slivers of orange gelatin (as sweet-and-sour sauce), and top with maggots (rice).

☠REGAN'S PEA SOUP☠ VOMIT (WITH BITS)

INSPIRED BY The Exorcist

Don't let this sweet and chunky version of pea soup make your head spin. It tastes much better than it looks. See page 38 if you're craving a savory pea soup.

Yield: 2 to 4 servings   Prep time: 15 minutes   Cook time: 30 minutes

DEADLY INGREDIENTS

MATCHA PUDDING

1½ cups (360 ml) unsweetened almond or oat milk

½ cup plus 2 tablespoons (150 ml) coconut cream

3½ tablespoons cornstarch

⅓ cup sugar

1 teaspoon matcha powder

1 teaspoon vanilla extract

MATCHA RICE CEREAL CHUNKS

1 (10-ounce, or 283-g) bag vegan mini marshmallows

¼ cup (60 ml) melted coconut oil

4 cups (100 g) crispy rice cereal

1 tablespoon matcha powder

1. To make the matcha pudding: In a large saucepan, combine all the pudding ingredients over low heat and stir continuously until the liquid thickens into a creamy custard.

2. Remove the pan from the heat right before the pudding gets to the desired vomit consistency and keep stirring for another minute or so until it does reach the desired consistency. Transfer to a heatproof container and let chill in the refrigerator.

3. To make the matcha rice cereal chunks: In a separate large saucepan, melt the marshmallows and coconut oil over medium heat, stirring frequently.

4. Add the crispy rice cereal and matcha powder to the pan, remove the pan from the heat, and stir to combine.

5. Wearing gloves, very loosely spread the mixture on a parchment paper–lined baking sheet. Pull the marshmallow into strings if possible. You will want it to look lumpy and chunky in the pudding "vomit."

6. Let the mixture cool to room temperature, then remove from the baking sheet and tear or chop into random, bite-size chunks, the stringier and odder looking the better.

7. To assemble, mix the pudding and chunks in bowls with a spoon and serve immediately. Try to aim for the grossest pudding-cereal ratio.

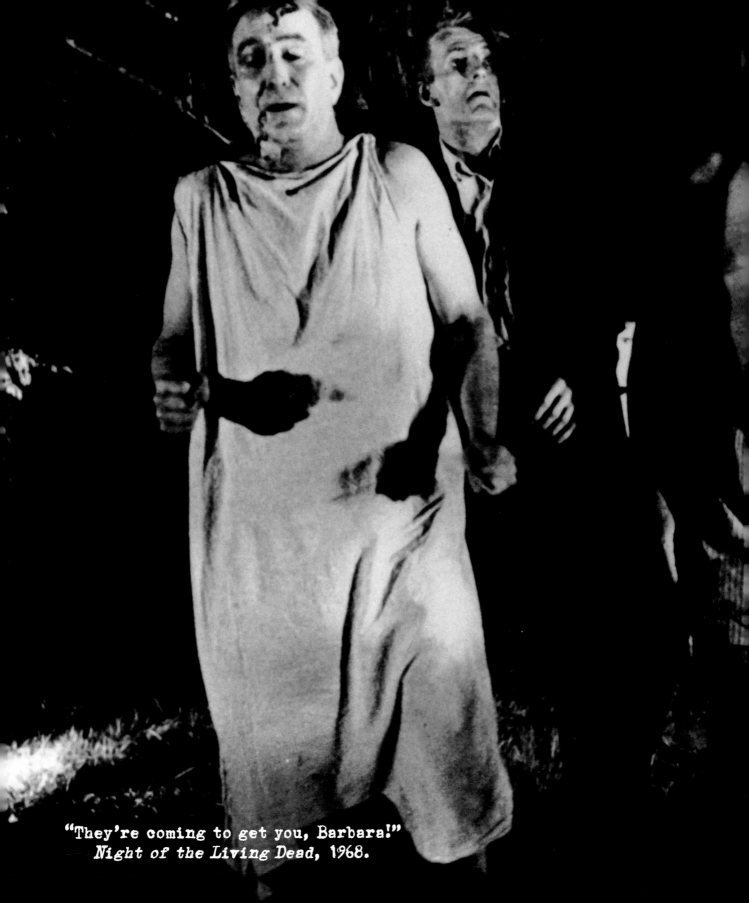

"They're coming to get you, Barbara!"
Night of the Living Dead, 1968.

 PIG'S BLOOD

INSPIRED BY *Carrie*

Mimicking the famous pig's blood scene in *Carrie*, this drink is made with black vodka, Grand Marnier, and cherry juice, which give it that perfect bloodred color.

Yield: 1 serving **Prep time:** 5 minutes

DEADLY INGREDIENTS

1½ ounces (45 ml) Blavod Black Vodka

½ ounce (15 ml) Grand Marnier

3 ounces (90 ml) cherry juice

½ ounce (15 ml) lemon juice

½ ounce (15 ml) champagne

1 blood orange wheel, for garnishing

1. Fill a cocktail shaker halfway with ice and add the vodka, Grand Marnier, cherry juice, and lemon juice. Shake well.

2. Pour the contents of the cocktail shaker into a collins glass, then top it with the champagne.

3. Garnish with the blood orange wheel.

CAPTAIN HOWDY'S MARTINI

INSPIRED BY The Exorcist

Take heed in how many of these martinis you consume, or you may very well will be seeing things! It tastes more innocent than it is . . .

Yield: 1 serving Prep time: 5 minutes

DEADLY INGREDIENTS

1½ ounces (45 ml) Hendrick's Midsummer Solstice gin

1 ounce (30 ml) melon schnapps

¼ ounce (7.5 ml) lemon juice

Dash salt

1. Add the gin, schnapps, and lemon juice to a cocktail shaker with ice. Shake well.

2. Strain the contents of the cocktail shaker into a martini glass.

3. Add the dash of salt.

WILLIAM PETER BLATTY'S

THE EXORCIST

Directed by WILLIAM FRIEDKIN

Something almost beyond comprehension is happening to a girl on this street, in this house and a man has been sent for as a last resort. This man is The Exorcist.

ELLEN BURSTYN · MAX VON SYDOW · LEE J. COBB
KITTY WINN · JACK MacGOWRAN · JASON MILLER as Father Karras
LINDA BLAIR as Regan · Produced by WILLIAM PETER BLATTY
Executive Producer NOEL MARSHALL · Screenplay by WILLIAM PETER BLATTY based on his novel
From Warner Bros. A Warner Communications Company

CRYSTAL LAKE

INSPIRED BY Friday the 13th

This unique take on an old-fashioned captures the essence of "camp" with sweet and bitter flavors, notes of campfire, and visual elements of blood.

Yield: 1 serving **Prep time:** 10 minutes

DEADLY INGREDIENTS

1 small slice blood orange, peeled

1½ ounces (45 ml) Irish whiskey (preferably Bushmills or Jameson)

1 ounce (30 ml) sloe gin

2 dashes aromatic cocktail bitters

1 smoking gun (or your favorite instant food-smoking device) (see Note on page 37)

1 large ice cube, for serving

1 blood orange rind, for garnishing

1. Place the peeled blood orange slice into a cocktail shaker or glass and muddle well.

2. Pour the whiskey, sloe gin, and bitters over the top of the muddled blood orange. Stir well.

3. Insert the tube of the smoking gun beneath the surface of the liquid and push smoke into it for 8 to 10 seconds.

4. Pour the contents of the cocktail shaker into a rocks glass over the large ice cube.

5. Garnish with the blood orange rind on top.

⇐ BILL'S TRU ⇒ BLOOD MARTINI

INSPIRED BY True Blood

This is a "truly" delicious spirit that looks and tastes as though you're living in a vampire drama yourself.

Yield: 1 serving **Prep time:** 5 minutes

DEADLY INGREDIENTS

1½ ounces (45 ml) vodka (preferably Grey Goose or Skyy)

1½ ounces (45 ml) Pama pomegranate liqueur

½ ounce (15 ml) sloe gin

1 slice blood orange, for garnishing

1. Add the vodka, pomegranate liqueur, and sloe gin to a cocktail shaker with ice. Shake vigorously for 30 to 40 seconds.

2. Strain the contents of the cocktail shaker into a martini glass.

3. Garnish with the blood orange slice.

KETTLE CORN COCKTAIL

INSPIRED BY Scream

Why eat kettle corn when you can drink it? Kettle corn-infused gin is the base for this cocktail with citrus to top it off. You'll constantly be "Craven" this drink.

Yield: 1 serving Prep time: 5 minutes (plus overnight infusing)

DEADLY INGREDIENTS

KETTLE CORN-INFUSED GIN

1 (750-ml) bottle gin

1 cup (19 g) kettle corn popcorn

COCKTAIL

1½ ounces (45 ml) kettle corn-infused gin

3 ounces (90 ml) orange juice

Dash orange blossom water

Kettle corn, for garnishing

Edible flowers, for garnishing

TO MAKE IT

1. To make the kettle corn-infused gin: Combine the gin and popcorn in a wide-mouth container. Cover and refrigerate overnight.

2. To make the cocktail: Fill a cocktail shaker halfway with ice and add the kettle corn-infused gin, orange juice, and orange blossom water. Shake well.

3. Strain the contents of the cocktail shaker into a coupe glass.

4. Garnish with the kettle corn and edible flowers.

BAY HARBOR BLOODY MOJITO

INSPIRED BY Dexter

A citrus and mint–infused cocktail with notes of coconut and a bloody finish for the full experience, this mojito goes down easy after a good kill.

Yield: 1 serving **Prep time:** 5 minutes

DEADLY INGREDIENTS

2 ounces (60 ml) white rum (preferably Bacardí Superior)

10 mint leaves, divided

1 ounce (30 ml) fresh squeezed lime juice

¾ ounce (22.5 ml) grenadine

1 ounce (30 ml) club soda

Crushed ice, for serving

½ ounce (15 ml) coconut rum (preferably Malibu)

1. Add the rum to a cocktail shaker with 5 of the mint leaves and muddle the leaves until well crushed to release the oils.

2. Add the lime juice, grenadine, and some ice cubes to the shaker. Shake well.

3. Put the remaining 5 mint leaves and the club soda in the bottom of a highball glass. Fill the glass halfway with crushed ice.

4. Strain the contents of the cocktail shaker into the glass over the ice. Stir a few times to blend.

5. Pour the coconut rum over the top.

⚙️ NEVER SLEEP AGAIN ⚙️

INSPIRED BY *A Nightmare on Elm Street*

Stay awake! In this take on an old-fashioned, the coffee keeps you up, the chocolate liqueur gives you a taste of celebration for staying alive, and the kick of whiskey and rum strengthen your courage to fight the demons.

Yield: 1 serving Prep time: 5 minutes

DEADLY INGREDIENTS

⅛ teaspoon vanilla extract

1 shot chilled espresso

1½ ounces (45 ml) Irish whiskey (preferably Proper Twelve)

½ ounce (15 ml) Godiva Dark Chocolate Liqueur (dark is dairy-free)

⅕ ounce (6 ml) black spiced rum (preferably The Kraken)

¼ ounce (7.5 ml) simple syrup

2 dashes aromatic bitters

Ice cubes, for serving

1 coffee bean, for garnishing

1 orange rind, for garnishing

1. Add the vanilla, chilled espresso, whiskey, dark chocolate liqueur, rum, simple syrup, and bitters to a cocktail shaker with ice. Shake well for 20 seconds.

2. Pour the contents of the cocktail shaker into a rocks glass.

3. Garnish with the coffee bean and orange rind.

 FIRE AND DREAMS

INSPIRED BY A Nightmare on Elm Street

This take on the Blood and Sand has a blend of scotch, vermouth, and cherry flavors that will immerse you in a dreamlike state while the tart blood-orange flavor wakes you up.

Yield: 1 serving Prep time: 10 minutes

DEADLY INGREDIENTS

1 ounce (30 ml) blood orange juice

1 ounce (30 ml) sweet vermouth

1 ounce (30 ml) cherry liquor

1 ounce (30 ml) scotch

Ice cubes, for serving

1 orange wheel, for garnishing

Sugar, for dipping

1. To make the cocktail: Add the orange juice, vermouth, cherry liquor, and scotch to a cocktail shaker with ice. Shake well.

2. Strain the contents of the cocktail shaker into a double rocks glass over ice.

3. To make the garnish: Dip the orange wheel in sugar, then use a kitchen torch to caramelize the sugar until it is melted and golden brown

4. Garnish the cocktail with the caramelized orange wheel.

NOTE

If you want to set your drink on fire, pour a little alcohol with 151 proof or higher over the orange wheel garnish in the drink and carefully light it. You can skip step 3 if you do this. (Be extremely careful when working with fire, and in this instance, fire mixed with a flammable substance such as alcohol.)

RICK GRIMES'S ULTIMATE WALKER JUICE

INSPIRED BY The Walking Dead

Gotta stay alert for the zombie apocalypse? This coffee drink will electrify your senses, get you ready to kill some walkers, and give you the courage to kick major ass all day!

Yield: 1 serving Prep time: 10 minutes

DEADLY INGREDIENTS

2 shots espresso

1 cup (140 g) ice

½ cup (120 ml) unsweetened nondairy milk

1 teaspoon vanilla extract

Agave syrup or sugar, to taste

2 ounces (60 ml) vanilla vodka (preferably Absolut)

Zombie Foam (page 111), for garnishing

1. Pour the espresso into a blender over the ice, then add the milk, vanilla, agave, and vodka. Blend on high for 1 minute, or until foamy and smooth.

2. Pour the contents of the blender into a glass for iced coffee.

3. Top with a healthy dollop of Zombie Foam.

ZOMBIE FOAM

INSPIRED BY Dawn of the Dead

Use this recipe to top off any of your favorite beverages, especially if you want to add some flair. This green coconut foam imitates the ooze that flows from the undead.

Yield: 1 serving Prep time: 10 minutes

DEADLY INGREDIENTS

1 (13.5-ounce, or 400-ml) can heavy coconut cream, extremely cold (refrigerate overnight or freeze for 1 hour before)

1 cup (125 g) confectioners' sugar

1 teaspoon natural green food coloring

½ teaspoon vanilla extract

1 teaspoon cream of tartar

1. In a large bowl with a hand mixer or the bowl of a stand mixer, beat all the ingredients on high until peaks form and the mixture resembles whipped cream.

2. Store in an airtight container and refrigerate for up to 1 week. If it becomes thin, mix it again to add air to make it fluffy.

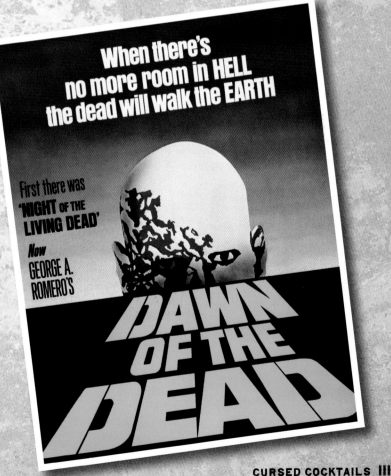

NORMA AND NORMAN (MOTHER'S MILK)

INSPIRED BY Psycho

What does a psycho drink? This cocktail from a bloody martini glass while calling for their dead mother.

Yield: 1 serving Prep time: **10 minutes** (plus cooling time)
Cook time: **15 minutes**

DEADLY INGREDIENTS

RIMMING BLOOD SYRUP

4 cups (800 g) sugar

½ cup (120 ml) light corn syrup

¼ teaspoon natural red food coloring

1½ cups (360 ml) water

MOTHER'S MILK

1 ounce (30 ml) butterscotch schnapps (vegan friendly)

½ ounce (15 ml) Gran Gala orange liqueur

½ ounce (15 ml) vanilla whiskey (preferably Crown Royal)

3 ounces (90 ml) vanilla almond milk
(or other vanilla-flavored nondairy milk)

I. **To make the rimming blood syrup:** In a medium saucepan, bring the sugar, corn syrup, food coloring and water to a boil over medium heat, stirring frequently. Continuing to stir, boil the mixture for 5 to 7 minutes until it reaches a thicker, syrupy consistency. Remove from the heat.

2. Dip the rim of a martini glass in the syrup and allow it to drip down the glass to make blood drips.
(Be extremely careful when working with boiling hot syrup, as it can stick to your skin and cause second-degree burns.) Let cool for at least 10 minutes.

3. **To make the mother's milk:** Add the schnapps, orange liqueur, and vanilla whiskey to a cocktail shaker with ice, then pour the almond milk over the top. Shake vigorously for 30 to 45 seconds.

4. Strain the contents of the cocktail shaker into the dipped martini glass.

 RED RUM

INSPIRED BY The Shining

"All work and no play make," well, anybody "dull"! So, take a load off and let Lloyd fix you a drink. The spiced rum will warm you up as that blizzard rages outside, while the ginger beer adds a refreshing spritz.

Yield: 1 serving **Prep time:** 5 minutes

DEADLY INGREDIENTS

1 ounce (30 ml) spiced rum

1 ounce (30 ml) sloe gin

4 ounces (120 ml) ginger beer

2 dashes aromatic bitters

1 splash of lime juice

Ice cubes, for serving

1. Add the rum, sloe gin, ginger beer, bitters, and lime juice to a cocktail shaker. Shake well.

2. Pour the contents of the shaker into a rocks glass over the ice.

THINGS COULD BE BETTER, LLOYD

INSPIRED BY The Shining

The red and yellow hues of this bourbon-based cocktail sweetened with cherries and maple syrup resemble the famous carpet of the Overlook Hotel. Red "yum"!

Yield: 1 serving Prep time: 5 minutes

DEADLY INGREDIENTS

3 pitted cherries, divided

½ ounce (15 ml) pure maple syrup

3 ounces (90 ml) bourbon whiskey

½ ounce (15 ml) fresh lemon juice

1 large square ice cube, for serving

1 lemon wheel, for garnishing

1. In a pint glass or the smaller half of a cocktail shaker, muddle 2 of the cherries with the maple syrup.

2. Fill the larger part of the cocktail shaker with ice, then add the bourbon and lemon juice. Combine the two parts and shake well.

3. Strain into a rocks glass over the large square ice cube.

4. Garnish with the remaining cherry and the lemon wheel.

⟦⟧TEXAS CHAINSAW⟦⟧
BLOODBATH

INSPIRED BY **The Texas Chainsaw Massacre**

The flavors of this Bloody Mary will get you revved up with its Texan twist and offers no escape once you taste it.

Yield: **1 serving** Prep time: **10 minutes**

DEADLY INGREDIENTS

3 dashes hot sauce of choice (preferably D. L. Jardine's Texas Kicker hot sauce)

½ ounce (15 ml) lemon juice

¾ ounce (45 ml) Chainsaw BBQ Sauce (page 122) or barbecue sauce of choice

5 ounces (150 ml) tomato juice

2 ounces (60 ml) vodka (preferably Tito's)

1 wedge lime

Mixture of course salt and freshly ground black pepper, for rimming the glass

1 jalapeño pepper, for garnishing

1 rib celery, for garnishing

1 lime wheel, for garnishing

1 lemon wheel, for garnishing

1. Moisten the rim of a pint glass with the lime wedge, then rim the glass with the mixture of salt and pepper. Set aside.

2. Add the hot sauce, lemon juice, barbecue sauce, tomato juice, and vodka to a cocktail shaker with ice. Shake well.

3. Pour the contents of the cocktail shaker into the prepared glass.

4. Garnish with the jalapeño pepper, celery rib, and lime and lemon wheels.

SPICY HITCHHIKER'S MARGARITA

INSPIRED BY The Texas Chainsaw Massacre

You don't have to go down South to enjoy a pristine margarita. Make this revitalizing beverage with a hint of Texas fire.

Yield: 1 serving **Prep time:** 5 minutes

DEADLY INGREDIENTS

2 slices jalapeño pepper

2 slices lime, divided

Splash of simple syrup

1½ ounces (45 ml) silver tequila

½ ounce (15 ml) Cointreau

½ ounce (15 ml) lemon juice

½ ounce (15 ml) lime juice

1 ounce (30 ml) orange juice

Course salt, for rimming the glass

Club soda

1 slice jalapeño pepper, for garnishing

1 lime wheel, for garnishing

1. In a pint glass or the smaller half of a cocktail shaker, muddle the 2 jalapeño slices and the remaining lime slice with the simple syrup.

2. In the larger half of the cocktail shaker, add the tequila, Cointreau, lemon juice, lime juice, and orange juice. Combine the two parts and shake well.

3. Pour (don't strain) the contents of the cocktail shaker into the prepared glass and top with club soda.

4. Garnish with the jalapeño slice and lime wheel.

"He has his father's eyes." Rosemary's Baby, 1968.

ATROCIOUS ACCOMPANIMENTS

☠ CHAINSAW BBQ SAUCE ☠

INSPIRED BY The Texas Chainsaw Massacre

Use this homemade barbecue sauce in place of your favorite store-bought version. Its uses are endless, even on headcheese . . .

Yield: makes about ¾ cup (100 g) Prep time: 5 minutes Cook time: 5 minutes

DEADLY INGREDIENTS

½ cup (68 g) ketchup

2 tablespoons brown sugar

1 tablespoon cider vinegar

¼ teaspoon sriracha sauce

1 teaspoon garlic powder

½ teaspoon mustard powder

½ teaspoon smoked paprika

½ teaspoon liquid smoke

1 teaspoon pure maple syrup

2 tablespoons bourbon whiskey

½ teaspoon ground cumin

1. In a medium saucepan, combine all the ingredients and stir over low heat until the mixture starts to bubble.

2. Allow the mixture to bubble, whisking or stirring constantly, for 1 to 2 minutes.

3. Remove from the heat and allow to cool.

4. Refrigerate in an airtight container for up to 3 months.

☠ CHAINSAW HOT SAUCE ☠

INSPIRED BY The Texas Chainsaw Massacre

Like to turn up the heat? You'll feel as though you are wearing a human-flesh mask once this homemade hot sauce makes you sweat.

Yield: about 6 tablespoons Prep time: **5 minutes** Cook time: **5 minutes**

DEADLY INGREDIENTS

2 tablespoons Tabasco

1 tablespoon sriracha sauce

¼ teaspoon cayenne pepper

2 tablespoons apple cider vinegar

1 teaspoon brown sugar

¼ teaspoon salt

1. In a small saucepan, combine all the ingredients and stir over medium heat until the mixture starts to bubble.

2. Remove from the heat and allow to cool.

3. Refrigerate in an airtight container for up to 6 months.

 TEX-MEX RANCH

INSPIRED BY From Dusk Till Dawn

Use this Southern-inspired ranch sauce with a kick at sunrise, sunset, or anytime in between.

Yield: about 2 cups (440 g) Prep time: 5 minutes (plus 3 hours resting time)

DEADLY INGREDIENTS

1½ cups (336 g) vegan mayonnaise

¼ cup (60 ml) unsweetened nondairy milk

1½ teaspoons apple cider vinegar

1 teaspoon garlic powder

1 tablespoon dried parsley

1 teaspoon dried dill

1 teaspoon Cajun seasoning

¼ teaspoon paprika

¼ teaspoon white pepper

½ teaspoon salt

½ teaspoon chili powder

⅛ teaspoon cayenne pepper

1 teaspoon agave syrup

1. In a medium bowl, vigorously whisk together all the ingredients for 3 to 4 minutes, until very smooth and well combined.

2. Cover and refrigerate for 3 to 4 hours for maximum flavor before using.

3. Refrigerate in an airtight container for up to 2 weeks.

 BEET KETCHUP

INSPIRED BY All Things Blood and Gore

Traditional ketchup is boring—and not the healthiest—so try this homemade beet ketchup instead. It's delicious, nutritious, and the perfect way to add "blood" to your meal presentations.

Yield: 2 to 4 servings Prep time: **15 minutes** Cook time: **30 minutes**

DEADLY INGREDIENTS

4 medium precooked beets

5 cups (1.2 L) water

¼ cup (60 ml) apple cider vinegar

½ teaspoon ground mustard

½ teaspoon white pepper

¼ cup (29 g) finely chopped red onion

⅛ teaspoon cayenne pepper

¼ cup (60 ml) soy sauce

½ cup (168 g) agave syrup

1. Combine all the ingredients in a food processor and process until smooth.

2. Transfer the mixture to a large saucepan and cook on low to medium heat for 20 to 30 minutes, stirring frequently, until thickened.

3. Remove the mixture from the heat and let cool.

4. Refrigerate in an airtight container for up to 1 month.

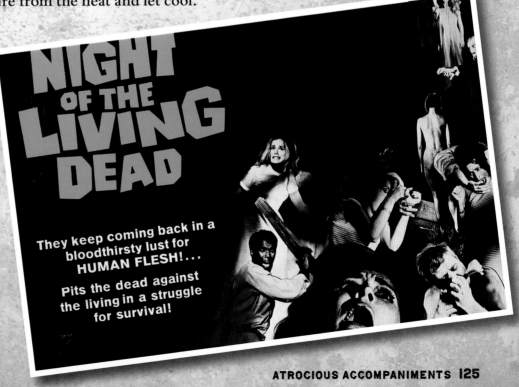

☠HELL SAUCE☠

INSPIRED BY Hellraiser

Not just destined for the Hell Burger (page 70), this sauce will add fire and brimstone to any sandwich. You can double or triple this recipe if you can take the heat!

Yield: 5 tablespoons Prep time: 5 minutes Cook time: 5 minutes

DEADLY INGREDIENTS

1 teaspoon cayenne pepper

½ cup (120 ml) Frank's RedHot or hot sauce of choice

1 tablespoon Tabasco

1 tablespoon agave syrup

½ teaspoon garlic powder

2 tablespoons (1 ounce, or 30 ml) whiskey

1. In a small saucepan, combine all the ingredients and whisk over medium-low heat until the mixture starts to bubble.

2. Remove from the heat and allow to cool.

3. Refrigerate in an airtight container for up to 2 months.

☠HELLFIRE AIOLI☠

INSPIRED BY Hellraiser

Don't be a pinhead! Pair this spicy aioli with burgers and sandwiches or use as a dipping sauce for fries and plant-based chicken nuggets.

Yield: about 3½ tablespoons Prep time: 10 minutes Cook time: 10 minutes

DEADLY INGREDIENTS

3 tablespoons vegan mayonnaise

1 teaspoon sriracha sauce

½ teaspoon agave syrup

¼ teaspoon garlic powder

Dash cayenne pepper

½ teaspoon Cajun seasoning

1. In a small bowl, whisk together all the ingredients thoroughly.

2. Refrigerate in an airtight container for up to 2 weeks.

 VEGAN BUTTER

INSPIRED BY Comfort Horror

Make everything "butter" with a vegan version of this recipe staple.

Yield: 2 to 4 servings   Prep time: 15 minutes   Cook time: 40 minutes

DEADLY INGREDIENTS

½ cup (120 ml) soy milk

½ teaspoon lemon juice

1 cup (240 ml) refined coconut oil

¾ cup (180 ml) light olive oil

½ teaspoon salt

2 teaspoons soy lecithin

½ teaspoon vegan butter extract

1. In a small bowl, mix together the soy milk and the lemon juice. Allow the mixture to sit without stirring for 5 minutes to create vegan buttermilk. It will curdle slightly.

2. In a small skillet, heat the coconut oil over low heat until it just barely melts. (It should not be hot.) Transfer the coconut oil to a blender, then add the olive oil, salt, soy lecithin, and butter extract, along with the vegan buttermilk. Blend on high for 1 minute.

3. Pour the butter mixture into a container (preferably glass) with a lid.

4. Freeze for 30 minutes, or until it is completely firm, then transfer it to the refrigerator, where it will keep for up to 2 weeks.

NOTE

You can buy soy lecithin online and at stores that sell nutritional supplements. Vegan butter extract can be purchased online and at some grocery stores.

 VAMP PASTE

INSPIRED BY **Dracula**

The garlic kick in this butter spread will not only keep the vampires at bay, but also make any dish "fang-tastic."

Yield: **about 2 tablespoons** Prep time: **5 minutes** Cook time: **5 minutes**

DEADLY INGREDIENTS

2 tablespoons Vegan Butter (page 127) or vegan butter of choice

½ teaspoon minced garlic

¼ teaspoon agave syrup

1. In a small microwave-safe bowl or saucepan, combine all the ingredients.

2. Melt in the microwave for 30 seconds or on a stovetop over medium heat for 2 minutes. Mix together well.

3. Keep soft or liquid for spreading onto bread to be toasted.

4. Refrigerate in an airtight container for up to 1 week.

NOTE
You can double or triple this recipe.

TRUFFLE GLAZE

INSPIRED BY **Giallo Films**

This earthy, rich glaze adds a touch of sophistication to dishes such as pasta, roasted vegetables, and salads.

Yield: **¾ cups (80 ml)** Prep time: **5 minutes**

DEADLY INGREDIGENTS

½ cup (120 ml) balsamic vinegar

¼ cup (84 g) agave syrup

Few drops truffle oil

1. In a small bowl, combine all the ingredients and stir well.

2. Put into a squeeze bottle or a container for spoon drizzling later.

☠ TOTALLY '80S CHEESE SAUCE ☠

INSPIRED BY '80s Horror Movies

It can be argued that the 1980s was the best decade—especially for horror films. Think gas-station-nacho-cheese-pumping goodness, except this take on nacho cheese sauce is less grotesque. There's no better way to indulge your '80s horror nostalgia than by putting this cheese sauce on everything. "Groovy."

Yield: 2 to 4 servings **Prep time:** 5 minutes **Cook time:** 15 minutes

DEADLY INGREDIGENTS

½ (13.5-ounce, or 400-ml) can coconut milk

5 slices vegan American cheese

1 tablespoon nutritional yeast

½ teaspoon sea salt

Pinch mustard powder

¼ teaspoon agave syrup

¼ teaspoon chili powder

¼ cup (30 g) Wondra Quick-Mixing Flour, or as much as needed for desired thickness

1. In a medium saucepan, combine the coconut milk, cheese slices, nutritional yeast, sea salt, mustard powder, agave, and chili powder over medium heat, whisking vigorously until melted and smooth.

2. Mix in the Wondra Flour to desired thickness.

3. Pour the cheese sauce into a bowl or gravy boat, or directly onto your dish.

4. Refrigerate in an airtight container for up to 1 week. Reheat in the microwave or on the stovetop.

SWEET ONION JAM

INSPIRED BY Goosebumps

There will be no unpleasant stench from this sweet and savory "goo." Onions become sweeter when cooked down, so don't be afraid of a harsh bite! Smear on sandwiches, serve with vegan cheeses and meats, and even use in pastries.

Yield: 2 to 4 servings Prep time: 15 minutes Cook time: 40 minutes

DEADLY INGREDIENTS

2 large sweet onions, chopped

½ cup (120 ml) apple cider vinegar

¼ cup (60 ml) olive oil

1 teaspoon salt

½ teaspoon white pepper

1 teaspoon ground mustard

2½ cups (600 ml) water, divided

½ cup (110 g) packed light brown sugar

1. To a medium saucepan, add the onions, apple cider vinegar, olive oil, salt, white pepper, ground mustard, and 1½ cups (360 ml) of the water. Stir to combine. Bring the mixture to a simmer over low heat, stirring occasionally, for 20 minutes.

2. Stir in the remaining 1 cup (240 ml) water and the brown sugar and continue to simmer for an additional 20 minutes, stirring frequently. If the mixture starts to get too thick or burn, add ½ cup (120 ml) more water. Let the water cook off. The consistency should be slightly syrupy and like a jam, not runny. Remove from the heat.

3. Let the onion jam cool, then transfer it to an airtight container or jar with a lid.

4. Refrigerate for up to 1 month.

💀 BLOOD AND BASIL SAUCE 💀

INSPIRED BY All Things Blood and Gore

This homemade red sauce is great on its own or add some vegan ground beef for a Bolognese like in Pastageist (page 72). Use for any recipe that calls for a tomato sauce.

Yield: 16 ounces (454 g) Prep time: 10 minutes Cook time: 3 hours

DEADLY INGREDIENTS

8 cloves garlic, minced

3 tablespoons extra-virgin olive oil

3 (28-ounce, or 494-g) cans San Marzano peeled tomatoes with juice

3 tablespoons sun-dried tomato paste

½ teaspoon each salt and freshly ground black pepper, plus more if needed

3 tablespoons finely chopped fresh basil

2 tablespoons finely chopped fresh oregano

1 tablespoon finely chopped fresh thyme

1. In a large saucepan, heat the 3 tablespoons olive oil over medium-low heat. Add the garlic and cook for 30 to 60 seconds, stirring constantly, until fragrant.

2. Add the canned tomatoes and their juices to the pan, followed by the tomato paste and ½ teaspoon each of salt and pepper and stir together. Let the sauce simmer on low heat for 3 to 4 hours, stirring every 20 minutes to avoid burning.
The sauce is ready any time after 3 hours of simmering.

3. When the sauce is finished, mix in the chopped basil, oregano, and thyme. Season with additional salt and pepper if needed.

☠CAMPFIRE☠ MUSHROOM BACON

INSPIRED BY Sleepaway Camp

This mushroom-based "bacon" is just as good as the real thing, and the spices and liquid smoke in the marinade may just remind you of your best (or worst) campfire memories.

Yield: 4 to 6 servings **Prep time:** 30 minutes (plus 6 hours marinating time) **Cook time:** 45 minutes

DEADLY INGREDIENTS

¼ cup (60 ml) olive oil

1 heaping teaspoon smoked paprika

2 heaping teaspoons brown rice miso

2 tablespoons pure maple syrup

1 teaspoon liquid smoke

1 tablespoon apple cider vinegar

½ teaspoon garlic powder

¼ teaspoon ground cumin

6 to 8 large portobello mushrooms, thickly sliced into long, bacon-like strips

1. In a large bowl, whisk together the olive oil, smoked paprika, brown rice miso, maple syrup, liquid smoke, apple cider vinegar, garlic powder, and ground cumin.

2. Add the sliced mushrooms to the bowl and toss until well combined. Let the mushrooms marinate in the refrigerator for at least 6 hours, or up to overnight.

3. When ready to cook, preheat the oven to 400°F (205°C; gas mark 6). Remove the mushrooms from the marinade and place them on a broiler pan. Reserve the marinade.

4. Bake for 35 to 45 minutes, until crispy (almost burned). Certain ovens may take longer.

5. Allow the mushrooms to cool in the pan, then brush them with more of the marinade.

☠ COWBOY CANDY ☠

INSPIRED BY *Bone Tomahawk*

The Old West is brutal, especially when you're dealing with a cannibal tribe. So, what better way to survive in the desert and keep those salivary glands busy than with these sweet pickled jalapeños.

Yield: 1 pound (454 g) **Prep time: 5 minutes** **Cook time: 8 minutes**

DEADLY INGREDIENTS

1 cup (240 ml) apple cider vinegar

2 cups (400 g) sugar

1 teaspoon celery salt

¼ teaspoon celery seed

1 tablespoon mustard seed

1 teaspoon garlic powder

½ teaspoon turmeric

¼ teaspoon white pepper

1 pound (454 g) jalapeño peppers, sliced (with seeds)

1. In a medium saucepan, combine the apple cider vinegar, sugar, celery salt, celery seed, mustard seed, garlic powder, turmeric, and white pepper over medium heat. Bring the mixture to a boil, whisking frequently, and boil for 2 to 3 minutes, until the liquid becomes syrupy.

2. Reduce the heat to low, add the jalapeño peppers, and simmer for 5 minutes.

3. Remove from the heat, pour the contents into an airtight container or jar with a lid, and refrigerate.

4. The cowboy candy can be refrigerated for up to 3 months.

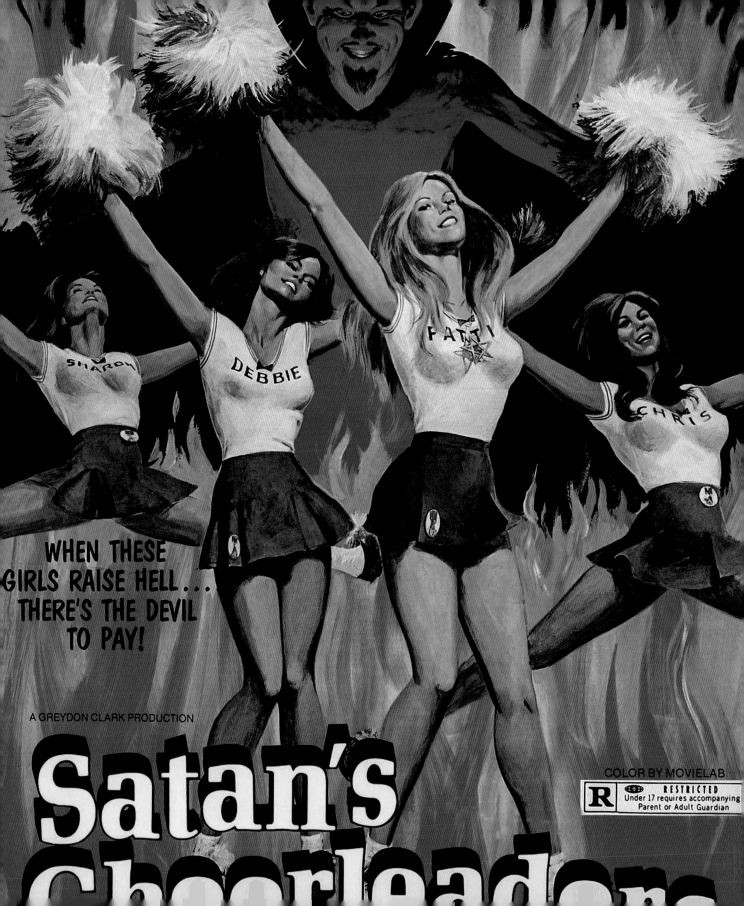

ACKNOWLEDGMENTS

Everything I have accomplished has been because of the amazing support and team I have around me. I thank God for the amazing life I have been blessed to live. Thanks to my family, friends, and the New Gold Empire crew for their constant support, including:

Gia Farrell, for badassery and recipe contributions.
Tim O'Grady, for behind-the-scenes photography and logistical support.
Sasha Natasha, for copy editing (without you, this book wouldn't have been completed).
Chef Chris Binotto, for recipe contributions.
Chef Chris Moulden, for recipe contributions.

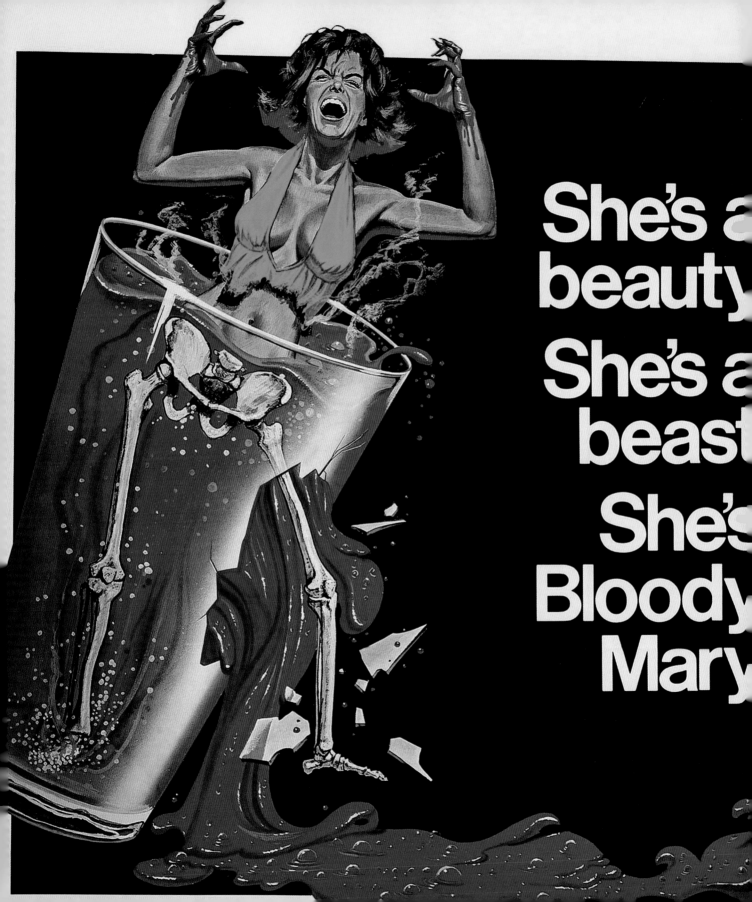

She's a
beauty

She's a
beast

She's
Bloody
Mary

RECIPE CREDITS

Chef Chris Binotto
The Hills Have Fries 24
Children of the Hominy 57
Haddonfried Steak 65
Pastageist 72
Blood and Basil Sauce 131

Chef Chris Moulden
All Hallows' Even Lasagna 59

Chef Annabel de Vetten Peterson
Blood-Soaked Loaf 85
Regan's Pea Soup Vomit (with Bits) 91
Sweet-and-Sour Maggots 95

Gia Farrell
Pig's Blood 98
Kettle Corn Cocktail 104
Things Could Be Better, Lloyd 115
The Spicy Hitchhiker's Margarita 107

Dan McDonald
Fire and Dreams 109
Texas Chainsaw Bloodbath 116

I WAS A
TEENAGE
WEREWOLF

ABOUT THE AUTHOR

ZACH NEIL is a self-made American entrepreneur, pop culture expert, musician, best-selling author, chef, and highly regarded business advisor. He owns or is invested in twenty-eight diverse businesses, such as restaurants, beauty brands, and tech platforms. Zach has been featured on the Food Network, *Good Day New York*, Cheddar News, Buzzfeed News, *Watch What Happens Live*, MSNBC, and ABC *World News Tonight*, and has graced the pages of *Maxim, Time, People, Esquire, Rolling Stone*, and many other publications. Zach's visionary ideas have gained him collaborations with the comedians Cheech Marin, on the new food concept Muncheechos, and Will Ferrell, on the Stay Classy pop-up bars. He's also known for his popular experiential entertainment programs, pop-up dining and drinking experiences, and, of course, his themed cookbooks!

INDEX